THE DISCIPLINE OF ENGLISH

THE DISCIPLINE OF ENGLISH

A Guide to Critical Theory and Practice

GEORGE WATSON

BOOKS
10 East 53d St., New York 10022
(a division of Harper & Row Publishers, Inc.)

First published in Great Britain 1978 by
The Macmillan Press Ltd

Published in the U.S.A. 1979 by
HARPER & ROW PUBLISHERS, INC.
BARNES & NOBLE IMPORT DIVISION

Printed in Great Britain

Library of Congress Cataloging in Publication Data

Watson, George, 1927–
    The discipline of English.

    Includes bibliographical references and index.
    1.   English philology—Study and teaching.
2.   Criticism—History—20th century.   I.   Title.
PE65.W3   1978   808'.042   78–12695
ISBN 0–06–497492–8
ISBN 0–06–497491–X pbk.

Contents

Acknowledgements   7

Introduction   9

Part One: The Critical Debate

1   Preliminary enquiries   15

2   Critics since 1920   25

3   Why literary judgements are objective   35

4   What history does   55

5   Language or linguistics   66

Part Two: The Tools of the Trade

6   How to read: or practical criticism   81

7   How to work: or using a library   95

8   How to write: or the use of English   106

Notes for Further Reading   119

Index   123

FOR

JONATHAN SMITH

Acknowledgements

This book arose out of a need to know more: twenty years of university teaching have kept me in a constant state of curiosity to learn how freshmen come to be as they are. A number of friends who teach English in schools, some of whom I first knew as undergraduates at Cambridge, have encouraged me over the years to visit them where they teach and to see for myself, and my first and most massive debt is to them. Some of the issues I raise here are wider than classroom teaching, and occasionally even wider than literature. But I could not have contemplated this task without the advice and example of those who, like my dedicatee, bear the burden and heat of the day.

My second debt is to St John's College, Cambridge which, among other indulgences, was a generous host to a teachers' conference on English in Schools in August 1975. And my third is to Derick Mirfin of Macmillan, who encouraged.

St John's College, Cambridge   G. W.

Introduction

This book is for those who teach and study English in upper schools with 'tertiary-level' studies in view, as well as in colleges and universities. Its main business is with what literary criticism does in the present age, and with what it can one day hope to do.

It appears at a highly delicate moment in education. In the 1960s, which some already call 'The Generation That Was Lied To', the young were told three tall stories: that you can command your native language, and even write it, with little or no systematic training; that literature is less a body of knowledge than a free-play area for personal judgement; and that there is a formula called the New Something which is about to solve the riddle of everything. An age of intellectual patent medicines, it was often more interested in the label on the bottle than in what came out of it. Above all, it was gullible of anything called new, even when its substance was old.

But much of what was then thought new, it is now clear, was nothing of the kind; and the educational spirit of the 1960s, though radical in rhetoric, now looks highly conservative in its effects. It entrenched comfortable prejudices. It is now reasonable to hope that the last quarter of the twentieth century will prove at once more radical in substance and more cautious in rhetoric. It is already marked by a spirit of critical rejection. There are parents who reject the prospect that their children should face the world without having been taught to read or write. There are the young themselves, resentful of the deceit that has been practised on them, who see permissive teaching as an easy excuse for teaching little or nothing. And there are taxpayers who reject the notion that they should sustain elaborate and expensive acts of intellectual self-indulgence.

The crisis has meant an awakening, and this book could hardly hope for attentive readers if many were not already alive to a sense of what teaching in a sympathetic atmosphere can achieve. I judge the present academic temper, like my own, to be sceptical of brandnames. The New Criticism that dominated much of Anglo-American criticism in the 1940s and 1950s, and likewise the *Nouvelle Critique* fashionable in France and elsewhere since the 1960s, can now be seen to have been highly conservative in the assumptions that sustained them. Though they proudly called themselves schools of criticism, they were schools for learning easy answers and parroting them back, and they were ill equipped to sustain any critical analysis brought to bear on themselves. Now that the vogue for easy answers is passing, it is becoming commoner to see literature as complex and of many kinds – and to respect it the more for refusing to yield its secrets all at once. This book is for those in English studies who want to work harder and look harder.

The first part of the book includes a review of the present state of things in critical theory: a task that strikes me as inescapable. But it leads to what must look like an imbalance between the first part and the second. I hope that the reader will excuse the contrast between arguments about advanced theoretical questions in the first part, and elementary information about reading and writing in the second. It reflects, after all, the needs of the time. Remote as the Age of Criticism (*c.* 1945–65) now seems to many young minds, it is not really possible to understand where academic English stands today without considering its period of gestation between the wars. It is what it now is because of the pioneers of the early and mid-twentieth century; and though we need not be grateful to them, and may even choose to resent them a little, we cannot simply be content to remain ignorant of how the subject was made. I remain unrepentantly convinced – as much as when I wrote *The Literary Critics* (1962) – that no one can know a subject if he knows nothing of its history, or misunderstands that history. And this book is explicitly designed for those who accept that English is a subject or 'discipline', and in the fullest academic sense of those words. For those who see it as a leisure activity – who are, I hope, many – it will seem oddly obsessed with questions about how literature has been taught and studied in this century. But that concern, after all, is proclaimed in its title. My readers are those who teach and study English in schools and universities, or who hope to do so, and I need no convincing that English has many other purposes than that.

Since literary criticism is a kind of literature, at its best, many of my arguments will concern literature at large as well as criticism in particular. Some of them may seem to run disturbingly beyond literature itself. That is because the very status of literature as knowledge is now under attack. The age now needs a new Apology for Poetry, a revised humanism, in the sense of a vindication of literature (including literary criticism) as a descriptive and truth-telling instrument. And all that can only be done in comparative terms. English urgently needs to be compared with other intellectual activities, and its certainties and practical utilities related to other subjects. This may lead at times to some dizzying plunges in argument, and remote analogies will sometimes be invoked here, including some from beyond literature itself. But any apologist for poetry will need a reader dedicated to patient reflection and to a concern as to whether argument is cogent – ready to follow where argument goes, even if it goes towards an eccentric conclusion. Criticism now needs to learn a new respect for reason and candour: that is what the New Humanism will mean. It matters that we should care that our arguments are good, and that we should publicly appear to care that they are so.

The first and longer part of the book, then, 'The Critical Debate', is designed to show that literary theory can be discussed in a manner at once rigorous and lucid. The second part, 'The Tools of the Trade', dealing with questions of how to read, work and write, is necessarily more elementary, and is meant to show how essential knowledge about such formal properties as syntax and metre can be acquired, how the resources of libraries can best be used, and how argument can be efficiently presented. Either part can be read first. The disparity between them is great, and some may think startling; but it reflects that odd mixture of sophistication and ignorance that often characterises the mind of the literary beginner, and never more than in the present age.

Part One

The Critical Debate

Any mental activity is easy if it need not take reality into account.

Marcel Proust

Saxpence reward for any authenticated case of intellect having stopped a chap's writing poesy! You might as well claim that railway tracks stop the engine. No one ever claimed they would make it go.

Ezra Pound

1   *Preliminary Enquiries*

There is not that good which concerneth us but it hath evidence
enough for it self, if Reason were diligent.

Richard Hooker

He who knows only his own side of the case knows little of that.

John Stuart Mill

Criticism is the debate by which literature survives. It is an enquiry
into one aspect of the human past. Spoken or written, it studies
poems, plays and novels in their place and time – even when time is
the present and the place is here.

In this part of the book I shall be concerned with how the literary
past is studied, and how some of the wider concerns of the age influence, for better or worse, what the critic does.

Some misconceptions are still widespread enough to be worth setting to rest at an early stage. They are best considered one by one, and
in summary form. Some will be enlarged on later in the book.

I

Criticism is still sometimes seen as a personal view, and nothing more.
In my third chapter I shall argue for its status as an objective enquiry:
one which is always more than a personal matter, even when it is most
plainly that, and one where questions of accuracy and inaccuracy
arise. If it were not so, after all, one could hardly speak of literary
judgements as being judicious, or personal, or prejudiced – all words
that imply a possibility of right answers and wrong ones.

The reflection is liberating. It means that even the greatest critic or
teacher can be wrong: it even opens up the possibility that he might be

shown to be so. And that realisation is crucial. Criticism can be original, creative and (in the last resort) subversive only because of its
claim to objectivity. If every man's literary opinion were as good as
anybody else's, criticism could hardly exist at all except as an enter-
tainment.

The subjectivist is one who believes that no perception is false, and
he is the mortal enemy of the critical spirit. Deliberately or not, his
view is ultimately at war with everything that criticism does or aspires
to do. He holds that literary differences can only end in agreements to
differ, and that in matters of taste there can be no rational dispute.
Though sometimes mistakenly espoused by radicals, subjectivism is
none the less a conservative doctrine, since it offers easy and endless
excuses to keep one's convictions as they are. It is bent on conserving,
and its claim to radicalism is spurious or unreflected. At its most characteristic, it insists that argument should conveniently stop to give
inclination free passage; whereas the critical spirit insists that argument should go on – even when, or especially when, it is disturbing in
what it unearths. And that insistence, or lack of tact, is its hallmark. It
is hostile to intellectual inertia, to the school of 'I know what I like',
and subversive of superstition: of any doctrine, old or new, that pro-
tects itself against uncomfortable evidence by refusing to look or by
pretending that it is not there.

II

Criticism is a kind of explanation. A highly social activity, much as
conversation is, it depends heavily on assessing whoever is likely to
read it or listen to it.

But any explanation that is harder to follow than what it affects to
explain has already failed. At its best, it is a waste of time and lacks a
reason to exist. That is why special terminologies, or polysyllabic
jargon-systems, need to be constantly challenged. They flourish,
when they do, as the secret or semi-secret languages of coteries
dominated by a cult of the personality that devised or adopted them;
and unless they can be shown to be indispensable, the motives behind
them are understandably suspect.

III

It is often tempting to shun the obvious and seek diversion in the
sophisticated. Much twentieth-century criticism is strenuously over-
ingenious, especially when confronted with such established authors

as Shakespeare. It forgets that Shakespeare was an artist of the popular theatre, and an accomplished master of the obvious. To neglect what his characters plainly say, or to interpret what they say in a contrary sense, is to cheat his plays much as the witches cheated Macbeth:

> And be these juggling fiends no more believ'd,
> That palter with us in a double sense.   (v viii 19–20)

Shakespeare's enormous subtlety is not in question. But that subtlety counts for little in isolation. It begins to count only in relation to a totality, and a totality that needs to be seen first and stated first. And the subtle, though it refines, cannot annul. Othello is noble, even though he behaves ignobly, and the play calls him noble because he is just that. Macbeth is a hero, even if a criminal too; Cleopatra a harlot, though not only that; and Juliet and Desdemona ladies of high virtue, if much besides. To lose sight of the obvious is to lose sight altogether, and the pea-and-thimble trick of seeing irony and symbolism on all sides no longer looks the game it once did. The great critical essay dares to begin with an assertion that is blindingly and self-evidently true.

IV

To study literature is sometimes thought useless, in the worldly sense, or at the best decorative. It is a deep assumption in our cultural life that the sciences and technologies are useful, the arts purely self-rewarding. The counter-case of supersonic aeronautics should give us pause. Few would defend Concorde on strictly practical grounds, though an engineer once called it 'the most beautiful thing I have ever seen'. Machines can be beautiful, and little else: poems can be ugly, and still poems. The difference between the arts and the sciences, then, whatever it is, cannot be aesthetic pleasure.

The claim that literature is useless, which is sometimes a righteous boast in thin disguise, may be countered in two ways: by showing it is false in its own terms, or by extending the concept of utility. If the study of English trains the mind, then it cannot be called useless – assuming only that modern societies need trained minds. But English is also the language of the world, and the first common language that educated mankind has ever enjoyed in its history. About three-quarters of the world's letters, as they pass through the mails, are now estimated to be in English. Even on the narrowest and most mercenary interpretation of utility, it can easily be shown that English is useful. Almost the whole world wants to know it, or to know it better. It could easily be a source of wealth and of political influence, and in some measure already is.

No one is under any obligation to want either power or wealth. That does not alter the fact that they are there for the taking. Any nation, and any individual, may choose to be weak or poor, and may even be right to do so; it is a choice both saints and sinners have knowingly made. But the truth remains that the demand for English is nearly as wide as mankind itself. There is a task for critics here, still largely unattempted, and one that could be useful in more senses than one: to demonstrate how literature can advance a knowledge of English as a second language in every continent.

V

Criticism is sometimes thought of as a mere auxiliary to literature, as literature to life. Neither assumption will bear much weight in argument. Much of life as we know it is already highly literary, in the sense that novels, plays and films massively influence ordinary behaviour. There is little enough in life as we know it that is 'raw'. And much literary criticism is itself literature, and sometimes great literature. Samuel Johnson was no less a man of letters in his *Lives of the Poets* than in his poems, or Henry James less of an artist in his essays and prefaces than in his novels. Criticism, at its greatest, is a kind of literature, just as poems and novels can in their turn be about literature. Sterne's *Tristram Shandy* and Coleridge's 'Kubla Khan' are works concerned with the difficulty or impossibility of writing *Tristram Shandy* or 'Kubla Khan', and these are critical questions. Many twentieth-century American poems are about how hard it is to write a poem; often enough, the poem that is being written. Criticism, in short, is not outside literature, but a part of it. It is a vital organ and not an adjunct.

VI

In the superstitions of many an *avant-garde*, it is established dogma that the old is never new, and that the works of past ages cannot help us. But if literature is to inform as well as to remind, then it can work all the more powerfully because it is remote. W. H. Auden once remarked that the aspect of Oxford English that most enriched his life as a poet over the years was its compulsory Anglo-Saxon. Poets, unlike some of those who study them, do not need to be told that what is alien is often of deeper creative value than what is already possessed. Keats's fervent enthusiasm for Shakespeare and Milton, poured out in his letters, demonstrates how instantly teachable and delicately impressible the mind of the poet is.

Literature stands under no absolute or continuous duty to be about ourselves. The otherness of other minds in remote ages may be as significant as their similarity, and it is not a matter for regret that mankind is various, unsubjugated by any single law of nature or of nurture.

A similar reflection applies to the history of criticism. There is a provincialism of time as of place, and those who begin every critical discussion as if the question had been invented yesterday betray an ignorance that is worse than merely technical. The great critics since Plato have considered so broad a range of issues that it is by now only sensible to assume few questions to start from scratch. The great critics can help, if we let them. It is disabling to begin every argument from its familiar beginnings with no sense of their familiarity, or to blunder through the early stages of a debate already well known to men of literary education. Aristotle never read a novel, but his account of 'mimesis' in the *Poetics*, or the imitation of reality, needs to have been mastered by anyone concerned with the problem of realism in modern fiction. What Johnson and Coleridge wrote about the objectivity of value-judgements counts, whether one agrees with it or not. Originality, it has been said, is the suppression of sources, and much of what is called new in critical fashion is mutton dressed as lamb – the dressing being a matter of terminology. That is one reason why intellectual history is an essential element in literary studies. Nothing is new for being called that, except to the gullible.

VII

To memorise, which is often supposed to be a purely mechanical exercise, is sometimes thought of as an inferior activity, especially since in literary circles 'mechanical' is an easy term of contempt. That is why fashions in teaching, which are still influenced by old-fashioned ideas which in the early twentieth century were thought progressive, still discourage learning poems by heart, or at the best fail to encourage it as they might.

The fear of memory is based on several misapprehensions: that it is a mere exercise, when in truth it is an opportunity for contemplation and intellectual growth; that it is a sordid device for passing examinations, though in fact many examiners despise frequent quotation, especially when delivered at length; that it is unrelated to critical intelligence, which is observably false; and that it has nothing to do with creativity. But any alert reader of a novel, or spectator of a play, needs to be able to remember certain vital elements in what he has read or heard. A literary historian needs a good memory to detect similarities between what he reads and what he has read, whether allusion, imitation or parody. And poets, who often have good memories, know how to prize it. Wordsworth, in his preface to *Lyrical Ballads* (1800), made recollection the source of poetic creation; and Keats, in a letter to a friend, proposed this plan as a way of life:

> Let him on a certain day read a certain page of full poesy or distilled prose, and let him wander with it, and muse upon it, and reflect upon it, and bring home to it, and prophesy upon it, and dream upon it, until it becomes stale – but when will it do so? (19 February 1818)

Memory is the most undervalued of all literary talents in the present age. The Greeks, however, made no mistake here. They called it the mother of the Muses.

VIII

There are those who fear that critical interpretations that are not moral are trivial. That is why many are content to be ignorant of formal properties like metre and syntax, imagining that to be able to tell a noun from a verb, or heroic couplets from blank verse, can only trivialise debate. Such formalities as these do not answer Matthew Arnold's insistent question about 'how to live', and there are those who think that question so urgent that it admits of no other. Formal ignorance can easily be tolerated, even encouraged, in such an atmosphere. This helps to explain the crippling obsession with thematic interpretations in Shakespearean studies, both in literary criticism and in the theatre.

There is no need to judge between the value of theme and form in literature, for the single and simple reason that we do not have to choose: the critic can concern himself with both. But an ignorance of the instruments with which the poet works, and above all of language itself, can be nothing short of fatal. To neglect the elements is to commit elementary mistakes. Some critics run before they can crawl. But they would be astonished, if they stooped to crawl for an instant, at the riches of language that are to be seen at close hand.

The insistently moral interpretation of literature since Arnold has been subject to a limitation of another kind. Much of it has lamentably lacked the rigour that moral analysis demands in its own right. It is not only poor criticism: it is poor when considered as ethical argument. By its very ambiguity it hopes to escape professional stricture, but debilitates itself in the process. Much of it is mere watered-down and anyone-can-play history of ideas, especially moral ideas, of a kind that would not begin to satisfy a competent intellectual historian. Arnold himself demonstrated a monumental ignorance of the intellectual sources of the English romantic poets, which he gravely underrated, when he depreciated them at length in his *Essays in Criticism* (1865–88), and his charge that 'they did not know enough' might justly be turned on himself. The terms 'Benthamite' and 'utilitarian' were commonly used in the pages of *Scrutiny* in a manner that suggested little or no acquaintance with the writing of Jeremy Bentham. The literary critic had better accept that, unless his training has run far beyond literature, he is an ignorant amateur in such matters.

Granted that the amateur has the right to exist and to express his views in the field of moral questions, if only because moral decisions are mandatory upon even the most ignorant of rational beings. But this is not a question of civic rights: it is one of professional competence. The critic who poses as a sage in these matters needs to be reminded that the study of moral philosophy is older than Plato and can show more proficient exponents than the critics of literature, in this century as in others. A critical essay is neither a sermon nor a moral treatise.

IX

Criticism makes men unequal, since it enables some to see further than others. This is true of any advanced educational activity. Any parent who makes an intelligent remark to a child is creating inequality. But there are those who fear and hate inequality; indeed much educational theory exists less to promote education than to level the conditions in which men live.

The grounds for levelling are moral, though hardly convincingly so. No one has ever demonstrated that equality of educational opportunity or provision, highly incompatible as they are with each other, are either of them compatible with social justice. That argument has still to be made; and mere assertion, however often repeated, cannot make it. This is an issue where conclusions are easily reached and passionately held, and it is the passion that makes for the ease.

If we could cease, for an hour or two together, to confuse equality with justice, and to consider the vexed question in a clear light, one conclusion would be irresistible: that criticism and educational equality are not to be reconciled. There are numerous practical reasons why you cannot give everyone an advanced literary education. When we teach and learn, in this academic field as in others, we are not merely condoning inequality but actively advancing it. Every university teacher advances inequality whether he knows it or not, and whether he admits it or not – assuming only that he performs the task for which he is employed. It is for egalitarians in education, of whom I am not one, to resolve that contradiction to their own consciences.

x

Fashion is the grand ringmaster of criticism in the present age. It accounts for more conviction or affectation than anything else. There are many who are mortally afraid of being thought unfashionable. That is why they adopt literary views after the manner of a well-dressed woman choosing her clothes.

Much of the intellectual fervour of recent years has been less for knowledge than for a sense of belonging to an *avant-garde*: a sort of literary version of Nazism, where views are cherished not because of any truth-content they are rationally thought to possess, but because of the collective hysteria they evoke. Universities are not chiefly to blame here – far less, certainly, than the mass media.

But when apparently intelligent and informed people believe in a single stereotype of nonsense, it is well worth asking why. Asking why is one thing that criticism does, and one of the things it does best. It analyses intellectual fashion, to destruction. If it is performing its own just function, then it is not itself swayed by a desire to appear fashionable; and it is unmoved by a fear of solitude or the ridicule of the modish. The fashionable intellectual, by contrast, loves to run in a pack. The several schools of New Criticism in our time have been just such packs.

The most vital difference of opinion in academies is not between radicals and conservatives. It is between those who seek exciting answers and those who seek true ones. This book is not for the excitable. It is for those who, like Elijah in the Book of Kings, listened for a sign not in wind, earthquake or fire, but in a still small voice. One natural effect of an education that continuously excites, or seeks to do so, is a lot of over-excited people. And excitement is an overrated state of mind – especially when it means that the virtues of the contemplative intelligence are forgotten. But it is in the gentle contemplation of literature, its tranquil recollection in silence and in empty passages of time, as in walking alone or waiting for a train or a bus, that the triumphs of the critical spirit are best to be won.

It is always possible, for all that, that the truth should sometimes excite.

XI

We fear disbelief and disagreement. But the first and last duty of a teacher is to be disbelieved by those he teaches; and if he achieves that, what he does in between matters all the more. If he seeks to impart a critical sense, then he cannot in reason demand that it should stop short of himself; and he cannot, unless arrogantly, suppose that what he says must pass unchallenged. Agreement, and above all instant agreement, is a symptom of pedagogic failure. In any debate, a point heard in acquiescent silence is commonly a point lost.

What a teacher of literature may reasonably demand is courtesy of dissent. Polite disagreement is the goal of all good teaching, as of much in civilisation itself. That is not just because courtesy is a good in itself. It is because it lets the argument run further, pierce deeper, and question more and ever more assumptions that have been cherished or accepted on insufficient grounds. It oils the wheels. It is not only a civilised good in itself, but an intellectual propellent. It makes argument go further and go better.

Disagreement is the highest intellectual flattery, then, and not an act of indiscipline. The most rewarding comment on a lecture or an essay would be 'I thought you got it wrong, and for these reasons . . .'; and the more closely argued the reasons, the greater the flattery. Not all views, after all, are worth disagreeing with, and few enough are worth disagreeing with in detail. A great critic, like Aristotle or Coleridge, is one whose views have risen to the dignity of a disagreement that has proved earnest, persistent and long. To disagree with such minds is in itself an education.

Criticism makes for irreverence. It is ultimately an iconoclasm, and knows no shrines for burning candles at. That is not because its instinct is merely destructive. It is because testing-to-destruction is how poems, like other things that mankind makes, are known and valued for what they are.

2   *Critics Since 1920*

A traveller who has lost his way should not ask 'Where am I?'
What he really wants to know is, Where are the other places? He
has got his own body, but he has lost them.

Alfred North Whitehead

We do not have to acquire humility. There is humility in us – but
we humiliate ourselves before false gods.

Simone Weil

In 1945 literary criticism stood near the peak of its fortunes in the
English-speaking nations. In the United States, even more than in
Britain, young men who had just returned to universities on the dec-
laration of peace found there a flowering of what was called the New
Criticism, and the prestige of English stood as high as that of any sub-
ject in the humanities.

Since the 1950s that prestige has declined. In this chapter I shall
trace that rise and decline in outline, though in no tone of regret. It is
not altogether good for a subject to be fashionable. And in later chap-
ters I shall consider how English, among other literary studies, might
find a place of its own to stand, and how it might recover some part of
its shattered fortunes.

The optimistic years that followed 1945 were marked by a doctrine of
literary study as the central discipline of advanced education. 'Central' here means that its relation with other subjects was supposed to
be a dominating one. English was held to have more to give to history,

social studies, psychology or linguistics than they to English. It was like the lord of a feudal court, surrounded by his vassals. That view, needless to say, was not always accepted by historians, sociologists and others. But it was a widely familiar view, accepted or not, and few in that era thought it merely absurd.

What does a subject need to be fashionable in an academic context? Three conditions, perhaps, need to be simultaneously met, and English in that age was felt to meet them:

1. centrality, or a claim to a dominating relationship with other and neighbouring subjects;
2. novelty, in the sense that a pioneering subject feels its achievements to be largely in the future, or 'watch this space';
3. a hidden conformity to the intellectual assumptions of the age.

To be new and yet conformist – conditions only seemingly incompatible – are properties which, in the event, can work harmoniously together. An intellectual fashion like the New Criticism in the 1950s needs to accept the world around it, and to take strength from that world: in this case a prosperous and largely contented society tired of violence, dedicated to the processes of patient analysis within an existing framework of debate, whether literary or political, and represented above all by a young generation of white, middle-to-upper class Americans avid for mental self-improvement. Modish radicalisms like the American New Criticism must confirm even as they deny; and a rhetoric of protest commonly masks a body of easy assumptions. A fashion, in brief, needs to swim with the current and somehow contrive to look as if it is swimming against it. Its collapse can follow upon the exposure of that paradox, when its assumptions are revealed by still newer and still younger critics to have been more ordinary, and more conformist, than their prophets had once supposed.

★

The critical boom that followed the Second World War, like the fashions for sociology and anthropology that came to displace it, precisely illustrates these principles. It is now common to call the two decades that followed the peace of 1945 the Age of Criticism. The American New Criticism, as it came to be widely known after John Crowe Ransom's *The New Criticism* (1941), was a school of formal and detailed analysis based on the Cambridge School that had flourished in England between the world wars. That school, in its turn, had been an act of discipleship to T. S. Eliot, whose poems and essays, such as *The Sacred Wood* (1920), had been cult-objects in the Cambridge of the 1920s. Eliot was an American who chose to live in London from 1914 till his death in 1965; so that the Cambridge School, as it may be called for brevity, was Anglo-American from the start, and the honours of its national origins need not be contested.

Its chief exponent in England was I. A. Richards, who was born in 1893 and became a lecturer at Cambridge in 1919. It was there, in the 1920s, that he invented practical criticism as a classroom activity, dominating Cambridge English until his emigration to Harvard in 1939. William Empson (b. 1906) was his pupil; F. R. Leavis (b. 1895), though never that, attended his lectures for years, and his periodical *Scrutiny* (1932–53) bears the stamp of his debt to Eliot and Richards, especially in its early years. As the Cambridge School turned into the American New Criticism in the 1940s, a long line of American academics and men of letters dedicated themselves in books, articles and classroom teaching to the new tradition of formal analysis of poetry: Ransom, Allen Tate, Robert Penn Warren, W. K. Wimsatt, Cleanth Brooks and many more.

The New Criticism was a lucid system based on a narrow range of assumptions, many of them characteristic of Anglo-American confidence in that age. First, it held that university English had more to give its neighbouring disciplines than they to it – a claim to centrality only sometimes accepted by others. Second, it believed that a close and attentive reading of English poems – and always poems rather than prose – in an analytical atmosphere, and with copious attention to their rhetorical properties, was new as an academic activity, and altogether the wave of the future: claims manifestly true, in their essentials, since English had only become a subject of any scope or scale in English-speaking universities after 1918. And third, the New Criticism silently accepted views concerning the nature of reading common in the years between the wars. The evidence for that does not altogether lie on the surface of things. Eliot was always a highly elusive critic in his public pronouncements; Richards, his younger friend and loyal academic disciple, was bolder and brasher in proclaiming where the future lay. But it was less what they declared than what they took for granted that shaped the critical school they made. These assumptions must now be exposed and considered.

In his academic training Eliot was a late Hegelian philosopher, schooled before and during the First World War at Harvard, Paris and Oxford. Richards, his junior by five years, had studied psychology at Cambridge. Neither had enjoyed a formal literary education beyond boyhood. It is in the nature of a new discipline, after all, that its pioneers are men who have been trained elsewhere.

Some of the consequences of these intellectual origins are of lasting interest. Eliot, Richards and the young Empson, who wrote *Seven Types of Ambiguity* (1930) as an undergraduate under Richards's guidance, all assumed that to read an English poem efficiently was to construe and explain a text in a manner familiar to anyone trained in Latin or French at school around the turn of the century. The New Criticism, at this fundamental and highly useful level, was an Old Pedagogy writ large. It was an attempt to professionalise English, and a successful attempt: to turn criticism from mere 'appreciation' and vapid enthusiasm towards a technique of analysis.

The attempt was of real benefit to early academic English. It taught thousands how to read; and it harnessed an existing analytical technique to the service of a new study. It underlies Richards's *Practical Criticism* (1929), a book based on experiments conducted in Cambridge classrooms through unidentified poems distributed to students and others for written comment. The comments or 'protocols' were then collected and arranged by Richards for critical analysis. Richards did not confine himself to students in that experiment: one of the unnamed authors of his protocols was T. S. Eliot. The names of poets were kept secret in order to discourage easy preconceptions and stereotyped judgements about periods and authors – an omission uncharacteristic of traditional literary explanation; so that Richards's experiment might better be called a preparative to the New Criticism rather than the thing itself. It was a technique for weeding out some of the damaging prejudices and facile generalisations that beset any study of a native literature.

The temper was cool, and some would have said frigid. Eliot's *Sacred Wood* had already been greeted by reviewers in 1920 as disturbingly analytical, and it was bound to look alien and exciting to an age taught to see poetry as a matter for romantic enthusing. Richards, in his turn, was soon to show how the clinical temper could be applied to the details of poems, even romantic poems. Empson and Leavis, as his successors, shifted the debate back into literary history, urging admiration for the verbal densities and ambiguities of the Metaphysical poets of the seventeenth century, to the disadvantage of most romantic, Victorian and Georgian poetry. If this caused some real injustice to the reputations of Shelley, Tennyson and others, and an eccentric emphasis on Gerard Manley Hopkins, it led to an even more dislocating effect: a neglect of the eighteenth century, largely unnoticed at the time, since that age presented a literature that offered few easy targets for praise or blame. The contrast between the School of Donne, on which Eliot had lectured at Cambridge in 1926, and the School of Wordsworth, was of too compelling an interest to allow much attention for those who had lived between.

The early training of Eliot and Richards had another effect on the New Criticism. Late Hegelian philosophy has to do with man's capacity to perceive reality; and F. H. Bradley, the Oxford philosopher who was the subject of Eliot's Harvard thesis of 1914, had laboured to construct a view that accommodated the extreme idealism of much of the nineteenth-century German mind, on the one hand, and some allowance for a perceived reality on the other. Man can in some distant sense know a real world through his senses, even if that knowledge is patterned by his individual mind. The idealist resolution of that dilemma was an uneasy compromise; and Eliot's *The Waste Land* (1922), with its half-despairing conclusion ('These fragments I have shored against my ruins . . .') and Richards's *Principles of Literary Criticism* (1926) are both anxiously balanced on a notional fulcrum between accepting and rejecting the possibility that man can perceive things as they are.

It is difficult, in this matter, to generalise about the stance of the Cambridge School. After 1930 it largely eschewed general questions, and did not call itself a school of practical criticism for nothing. But it is a reasonable summary of that view to suggest that 'the common pursuit of true judgement', a phrase of Eliot's to be adopted years later by Leavis as a title, implied a concern for the individual response to literature as much as a concern for literature itself. Practical criticism was increasingly a doctrine of true-for-me rather than true-absolutely: it was in that sense that its disciples found it liberating. They saw it above all as a doctrine of individual response, as opposed to an inferior brand of knowledge acquired at second hand out of handbooks. The task of the teacher, in this view, came to be seen as one of eliciting an awareness already latent in the pupil, and a sort of penetrative sincerity was held to be a validating principle.

Much of this accords with Richards's early interest in psychology.

In *Practical Criticism* it is above all the response of the student to the poem that matters; not in the sense that his response is always acceptable, but in the sense that it always holds the centre of interest. Richards rarely analysed poems himself, at least in print, and his published criticism usually stops short of the poem itself. An ideal response is hinted at, but no more than that, by quoting comments that are plainly something less than ideal. A student's response can be mistaken, to be sure: but because he has allowed certain acquired faults such as sentimentality to block the path to true understanding. The ideal object of practical criticism in its earliest form was pure confrontation between the mind of the poet and the mind of the reader; information, including historical and biographical information, being as much a hindrance as a help. And a concern with response is highly characteristic of the psychologist. Past events matter in psychology to the extent that they have affected the mind of the patient. The Cambridge School, in that sense, was an 'affective' school: it was concerned with the impact of poem upon individual mind, and response was the object of its profoundest attention.

In the *Scrutiny* critics of the 1930s and after, the Cambridge obsession with response was to grow, as it can easily grow, into a moral obsession. As attention moved from poetry towards fiction, and especially towards 'the great tradition' of English fiction from Jane Austen to D. H. Lawrence, a faulty response was readily felt to imply a moral defect. The *Scrutiny* critics were an Elect, like the Cromwellians, and aspired to a Rule of the Saints. Harshly puritanical noises arraigned a civilisation which, as they claimed, lay under an imminent threat of moral collapse. The menace of pornography, of which they espied hints in some unlikely places, haunted their minds and consciences. Eliot, Richards and Empson were not prepared to follow them into these strident fanaticisms, and were duly anathematised. By the 1940s a school was breaking up in a fervour of heresy-hunting.

And yet the Cambridge critics, and their successors the American New Critics, never abandoned a claim to know literature itself, or at least to be on the point of knowing it. This was an area of contention to be explored only late in the life of the school. A controversial article of 1946 by W. K. Wimsatt and M. C. Beardsley on 'The Intentional Fallacy' (revised in Wimsatt, *The Verbal Icon*, 1954) denied that the intention of the poet was either discoverable or worth discovering, but it did not go to the length of suggesting that only the response of the reader counts. All this echoes across two decades Richards's pronouncement in *Science and Poetry* (1926) that the thought-content of great literature is commonly overestimated. 'It is never what a poem *says* which matters, but what it is' (ch. 2). 'Never' is a confident word. But then theorising had not been trumps in the game of the New Criticism. They had been practical men, and above all practical teachers: it was not for them, as they saw it, to follow the argument where it led.

That abandonment of responsibility to the argument was, in the end, to prove costly. What is the thing that the poem 'is'? Not its thought, if Richards was to be believed; and not the poet's intention, if Wimsatt was. A tissue of structures, ironies, paradoxes and tensions, if Brooks and Penn Warren were to be followed. But these are often as much ways of seeing as things seen; and they can depend on where, as a reader, you happen to be standing. When literary subjectivism was revived in an extreme form in California, Paris and the German universities in the 1960s, in an atmosphere of defiant militancy, the Cambridge critics had only few and feeble arguments to answer it with. The militant, to parody his position, believed that everybody's opinion was as good as everybody else's, especially his own. That extreme had never quite been the view of the Cambridge School. But they were in no mind to answer it in any radical spirit. As a school of response and individual sincerity – 'What, dear boy, does Shakespeare mean to *you*?' – they had already sold the pass to an army of subjectivists that marched easily through. It is even a question of whether, by then, anyone much wanted to keep them out.

★

The New Criticism did not collapse suddenly on either Atlantic shore. It was a victim of attacks from more quarters than one from the late 1950s, and there were attacks which its ageing leaders sometimes contrived to absorb. It suffered erosion, not sudden death; and it could sometimes welcome competing studies into itself, such as the history of ideas, and suffocate them in a warm embrace. But it died, none the less, in the 1960s, its leaders already famous and replete with worldly success, untired of expounding their yellowing convictions before youthful if unsympathetic audiences. That slow erosion represents, in effect, the history of criticism in the most recent generation of Western man. It occurred in stages.

First, literary history revived, and the Cambridge School had been disdainful of literary history. Disdain is something less than contempt, and very remote from fear or hatred. But then you do not despise, fear or hate what you imagine to be dead or moribund. Eliot's early essay 'Shakespeare and the Stoicism of Seneca' (1927) (in his *Selected Essays*, 1932), a delicately derisive parody of a literary-historical essay in the Victorian or Edwardian mould, strikes a note that was to sound through the annals of the Cambridge School. The literary historian was supposed in that era to be a man of laughably limited and largely outdated function. He might write chronicles, as George Saintsbury had done, useful enough in providing beginners with a map of what there is to be read, and conveniently signalling the order in which texts were written. Or he might be a dry specialist, obsessed with sources and analogues and composing well-footnoted articles for learned journals. Eliot, Richards and their disciples never wrote chronicles or specialist articles, and they seldom read them. They would have thought that outside their duties and dignities as critics, if not beneath them. And that disdain for literary history, which in their disciples sometimes grew into arrogance, was in the end to cost them dear. Because they did not bother with historical questions or read periodicals, their understanding of the literary past rapidly came to look old-fashioned and erroneous. Leavis was not allowed to forget he had once praised, as a notable instance of Henry James's early mastery of fiction, a novel recast by that novelist in his sixties. The study of the past had more surprises to offer than they had imagined: it was nothing like as dead as they thought. Arthur Lovejoy's *Essays in the History of Ideas* (1948) studied intellectual ancestries in a manner professionally based on a revived technique of nineteenth-century German historical scholarship; medieval and Renaissance studies widened in the 1960s to include iconography and the relations between the arts; political and social history transformed the study of fiction in the wake of pioneer works like Humphry House's *The Dickens World* (1941); and Northrop Frye, in his *Anatomy of Criticism* (1957), showed new and idiosyncratic possibilities in an historical study of the literary kinds or genres, categorised in a work that was to enjoy a brief but intense vogue in the early 1960s. Meanwhile the application of intelligence to literary history, on a world view, had never, in truth, stopped or even taken much pause: Lionel Trilling's finest essays of the 1940s, collected in *The Liberal Imagination* (1950), encompass intellectual history and comparative literature in a style redolent of the cosmopolitan intelligentsia of New York. The

Cambridge School and the American New Critics, fundamentally incurious as they were in their critical writings about new historical knowledge, and resolutely introspective in their mental habits, were ill prepared for the survival or revival of literary history. The past had astonishingly awakened once again.

Second, literary subjectivism revived in the 1960s and after, most noisily and dogmatically in the *Nouvelle Critique* that flourished in Paris after the collapse of revolutionary enthusiasms in 1968. The *Nouvelle Critique* was a school of competitive subjectivism. It had begun in a mood of confident and often Marxist conviction that reality exists and can be studied, and that the urgent duty of mankind is to change it. By the end of the 1960s, such leaders of opinion as Roland Barthes had already come to doubt that literature can be seriously descriptive of reality, even when it is social fiction. They had even come to doubt reality itself. 'Be realistic: demand the impossible', a slogan painted on walls in 1968, began its life as an expression of radical determination, but it soon came to represent an increasingly surrealistic and unpolitical attitude to the business of life. If literary realism is a false pretension, not a fact; if literature does not, and even cannot, describe reality; if, as Barthes claimed, it is necessarily and always an 'art of disappointing', forever claiming to inform without ever in truth doing so; then the justification next to be made in its defence appeared to be that it creates structures within the minds of those who read. But even those mental structures, like as not, are merely individual. Can any given novel or 'text' – a cult-word of the Parisian school – be said to require, or even strongly to recommend, one such mental structure rather than another? The argument peers down a long, dark subjectivist tunnel, and the last stop in that tunnel is called solipsism. And a solipsist is one who believes there is no certain reality but his own mind.

The survivors of the Cambridge School were ill equipped to meet such arguments. That is not because, as arguments, they are very formidable; or because the Cambridge School tried to meet them and failed. It is rather because Cambridge, being itself a school of literary response, was itself more than a little subjectivist. It had never conceded an unimpeachable reality to literature itself, but only to what the reader could be trained into making of it, above all as an educational device. 'The touchstone is emotion, not reason', as D. H. Lawrence had put it in his essay on Galsworthy:

We judge a work of art by its effect on our sincere and vital emotion, and nothing else. All the critical twiddle-twaddle about style and form, all this pseudo-scientific classifying and analysing of books in an imitation-botanical fashion, is mere impertinence and mostly dull jargon. . . . The more scholastically educated a man is generally, the more he is an emotional boor.   (*Phoenix* [1936] p. 539)

Education was to be a training of individual emotion, and scholarship was almost a dirty word. No wonder, then, if the Cambridge School proved weak under the attack of a new and more extreme Parisian subjectivism. It had already accepted much of that case. It is even possible, though the matter is yet to be documented, that the *Nouvelle Critique* was historically indebted to the American New Critics; and that its extreme subjectivism, as a matter of intellectual influence, is ultimately an inheritance of the Cambridge School, though it also owed much to such post-war French philosophy as Sartre's. Since neither school of New Criticism, Anglo-Saxon or French, is remotely interested in questions of historical influence, and since all movements that call themselves new have an evident stake in claiming to be unique and original, the question of ancestry is unlikely to be studied, and then only by an outsider.

But the heritage of the new criticisms since 1920 now looks a sorry spectacle. They have left behind them a devastated area. Much of the most fashionable criticism in the Western world since 1968 has based itself on an extreme insistence that poems, plays and novels have no independent reality in themselves, that they do not and cannot describe any reality outside themselves, and that the critic in his turn cannot seriously hope to describe them. These are surely odd and self-defeating insistences on the part of any literary critic. They amount to a death wish. If that is what criticism does, then what criticism does is not worth doing. Such is the pass that subjectivism has brought us to.

In my next chapter I shall consider how to escape from it.

3 *Why Literary Judgements are Objective*

[If] the principles of our actions have no other support than our blind choice, we do not really believe in them any more. We cannot wholeheartedly act upon them any more. We cannot live any more as responsible beings.

Leo Strauss

If there were a verb meaning 'to believe falsely', it would not have any significant first person, present indicative.

Wittgenstein

In the 1960s literary subjectivism, which had never quite died, revived in full force.

Subjectivism is the doctrine that no perception is false; that judgements are altogether personal; that questions of taste differ radically in logical status from questions of fact; and that reason cannot adjudicate between opinions. *De gustibus non disputandum*; or, in a familiar phrase, 'I know what I like', with its common implication that no mere argument can alter my opinion.

Since the 1960s that issue has been more active and embittered than at any other time in this century; it threatens, as it is meant to threaten, the entire status of literary studies. If literary subjectivism were true, then it would be doubtful if English could rightly be called a study or a 'discipline' at all. To study something can only mean to study 'some thing', a body of knowledge yet to be acquired. If no perception in literary studies is false, then the word 'knowledge' can hardly apply to it. The only reply to Tolstoy, who thought Shakespeare a poor dramatist, would be a disagreement to differ: each to his own opinion . . . But knowledge cannot be pursued in that spirit.

That is why subjectivism threatens not just any given step in critical activity, but all criticism whatsoever. They are forever at odds. And this is true in practice as well as in theory, and it suggests an instant paradox: that there are those teaching and studying English in schools and universities, or claiming to do so, who do not in truth believe it to be an object of study. That state of affairs is plainly too precarious to last. Why, many will ask, if it is not an object of study, should it be pursued at all in a place of study, and at the public cost?

In this chapter I shall present reasons for thinking literary criticism objective, and for accepting the study of English and other literatures as a cognitive activity governed by rational procedures.

★

'Objective' in this context does not mean provenly true, still less certainly or indisputably true. To assert that enquiries into judgements like 'Shakespeare was a great dramatist' are objective is to assert that such judgements are true, or false, or partly true and partly false (great in this sense but not in that . . .). Whether, in a given state of knowledge, one can ascertain which of such judgements is true is a further question, or one of verification; and whether sufficient reasons can be efficiently stated is a further question again. To call a question objective is to make an assertion about its logical status, and it does not necessarily involve a claim to know the answer. The physical composition of the planet Neptune, for instance, is an objective question, even though physicists and astronomers do not know, or do not certainly know, what that composition is. That means that it is whatever it is independently of whether mankind, in a given state of knowledge, knows what it is or not.

Subjectivism is in no way a new doctrine, whether as a general proposition about knowledge or within the field of literary studies. But it has recently grown a new skin and made a fresh claim to be fashionable. This is why I speak of its revival. Protagoras, who lived before Socrates, spoke of man as the measure of all things, a remark often thought to signify that judgements are always relative to the individual that makes them. Bishop Berkeley, early in the eighteenth century, accepted Locke's challenge that knowledge is acquired only through the senses, and threw down a still bolder challenge: how then, if at all, do we know the real world to exist? Sterne's *Tristram Shandy* dallies wittily with this challenge, especially in those figures like Uncle Toby who live in mental worlds of their own devising. Positivists of the early and mid-nineteenth century often insisted on a total disjunction between questions of fact, which they accepted as objective, as in the experimental sciences, and questions of value, which they saw as personal and unverifiable. And the Logical Positivists of the Vienna Circle in the 1920s restated the doctrine with a firmer emphasis on truth as verification-by-experience; A. J. Ayer's *Language, Truth and Logic* (1936) is a philosophical treatise in this tradition. Meanwhile Marxist theories about conviction as an effect of social conditioning, which can easily be turned to subjectivist account, are as old as the 1840s and a by-product of still earlier views.

Recent literary subjectivists have not shown much interest in Protagoras or Berkeley, probably because they are anxious to look modern. They have shown an active interest in Marx, however, whom they oddly regard as a recent author. Active but selective: no Marxist, surely, has ever allowed himself to suppose that Karl Marx himself believed in social conditioning because he had himself been conditioned into believing in it. Every religion has its miraculous exemptions. But Positivism, that highly and conveniently portable creed, is still active among modern subjectivists, perhaps because it is so portable. Everybody who has not thought steadily on the matter believes he can easily tell a question of fact from one of value, and it is convenient to be told that they are of radically different status. The modern subjectivist, in practice, is often a neo-positivist, and he often sprinkles his arguments with Marxist jargon. It must seem odd that an *avant-garde* should have contented itself with a doctrine well over a century old. But the truth has to be faced: literary critics of a fashionable stamp are inclined to wear secondhand philosophical clothes with an air of chic. It is as if they had shopped in charity bazaars for goods marked down as 'Nearly New'.

Objectivism is often felt to be authoritarian, and supposedly threatens the liberty of the individual. It is strikingly common among those who adulate foreign dictatorships to be earnestly protective of individual liberty in schools and colleges at home. But a horror of authority still needs to be understood if one is to explain how intelligent and reflective men can accept the arguments of subjectivism, and why they anger so easily when the weakness of those arguments is exposed. They believe in them, above all, because they desperately *want* them to be true. They imagine that objectivism, whether in moral or in aesthetic judgements, would require everyone to believe the same thing:

a prospect they rightly feel to be intolerable. They have not yet understood that freedom of personal judgement is greater on the objectivist
assumption than on any other.

★

Literary subjectivism is based on a series of arguments which I shall
consider, broadly speaking, in order of sophistication.

  1. *The 'experts disagree' argument.* In a literary context, this means
that professional critics often disagree, and fundamentally. To make
the instance more telling, suppose that the two critics who disagree
fundamentally about a poet – Milton, as an example – have no extra-
literary axe to grind; or none, at least, that bears directly on their disagreement.

  The argument between T. S. Eliot and C. S. Lewis on *Paradise Lost*
may be considered as a paradigm here, the more so since both critics
were Christians, and indeed Anglicans, at the time of the controversy
that culminated in Lewis's *A Preface to Paradise Lost* (1942). Their disagreement was about Milton's greatness as a poet, which Eliot had
publicly slighted, and not about divine providence; and it was about
what doctrines the epic propounds, not about whether they are true or
false. It was a debate about Milton's grand style and his understanding of the Trinity and the Atonement, and it illustrates some
crucial considerations.

  First, experts often disagree about facts. It is a factual question
whether *Paradise Lost* is or is not an Arian poem – whether it denies
or asserts the divinity of Christ. So factual disagreements often
happen among experts; and not only in literature. Physicists often
disagree about the facts of the physical world, and economists about
the state of the economy. And the disagreements of economists are in
no way confined to questions of policy, which one could accept as a
matter of value. (Policy, after all, depends on what you want.) They
also disagree about such factual questions as whether incomes in a
given country have or have not tended to grow more equal over a
given period of years. If expert disagreement is to be accepted as evidence that the question is subjective, then we should have to conclude that many factual questions are subjective: a conclusion
unacceptable to the neo-positivist mind, though there are those engaged in the philosophy of science who toy with the notion. That
experts should disagree about literature, then, as Eliot and Lewis

once publicly did, is doubtless compatible with subjectivism, but it does not require it as a conclusion. And the nature of their disagreement is incompatible with a subjectivism that applies to value-judgements alone.

Second, it is sometimes supposed that it is facts that are agreed on, at least among experts, and judgements of value that are not. This can sometimes be so: Eliot and Lewis were agreed that Milton was a Puritan, and that *Paradise Lost* first appeared in 1667, even as they disagreed about its value as a poem. But this instance too fails to support the positivist case. For though the two critics were agreed that Milton was a Puritan, they were not agreed that *Paradise Lost* was a Puritan poem: Eliot believed it was, and Lewis argued that its Christianity was almost totally traditional. And the question of whether or not it is a Puritan poem is a factual question. Given the scale of the epic, it is a factual question of enormous complexity. But then factual questions often are of enormous complexity, and none the less factual for that.

For a counter-case to literary positivism, one could hardly do better than to recall the Homer problem. Experts have long disagreed as to whether the Homeric poems were written by one man or by more than one – a factual question. They have rarely, if ever, disagreed that they are great poems – a value-judgement. In the case of Homer, then, the question of value is agreed and the question of fact is not. The difference between questions of fact and questions of value, then, whatever it is, cannot be the same as a difference between what is agreed and what is not.

The case of Homer gives rise to another reflection: that one of the strengths of positivism, though a deceptive strength, is that some of its assumptions have by now entrenched themselves in the ordinary usages of language, and so deeply that they now appear to validate this aspect of the positivist case. When people say 'That is a matter of opinion', they commonly mean it is a matter on which reasonable people might reasonably differ; and when they say 'That is a fact', or 'The fact is that . . .', they commonly imply that only an ignoramus or a madman would deny it. Subjectivism is now buried deep in our ordinary speech habits, and this makes it the easier, at convenient moments, to revive. Those who acquiesce in this use of language often need to be reminded that facts can be wrong as well as right and disputed as well as certain; and that opinions can be true and proven as well as uncertain or false.

2. *The 'impressionistic' charge.* Literary criticism is sometimes called impressionistic, and in a sense meant to be damaging. And it is undeniable that critics have impressions of poems, and report them. So, for that matter, do experimental scientists have impressions of what they observe in their laboratories, and report them. But the charge of 'impressionistic', which sounds so much graver than it is, implies something more than this, and more derogatory: vague, smudged, lacking in clear outlines, evasive of verbal definition, un-equipped with a precise terminology, and the like.

But even the vaguest of impressions may, after all, be accurate; and all the more accurate for being vague. Not everything in nature or art is clearly outlined. The Sahara desert, which undoubtedly exists, has no precise border; and the more precise the border one were to draw for it, the less accurate it would necessarily be. Precision is not the same as accuracy, and can well be incompatible with it. In art an absence of precision, like the *estompé* or blurred effect of certain paintings, can be an essential part of its artistic effect. To call something imprecise or even indescribable may be a significant way of describing it accurately; if it were describable, after all, in the usual sense of being briefly and exactly describable in words, then it would be another and very different thing. If someone were to remark 'Something indescribable happened to me this morning', this would be a highly descriptive remark, in the sense that it would sharply delimit the range of possibilities within which that event could be placed; one could not, for instance, conclude with 'I had my hair cut'. The dramatic effect of the knocking at the gate in *Macbeth* might reasonably be called indescribable, and no less so because De Quincey in a famous essay ('On the Knocking at the Gate in *Macbeth*,' 1823) once made a bold and speculative attempt to describe it. We often try to describe the indescribable, and for good reason.

Poets often do so too. What is more, they sometimes emphasise, and in the poem itself, that they are attempting the impossible. Nobody thinks this a reason why they should not try; and since literary criticism is a kind of literature, the same tolerance might be allowed to critics. 'The thoughts expressed in music are not too vague for words', as Mendelssohn once remarked, 'but too precise.' Criticism of the arts often presents an intractable problem of description, and so does poetry. Medieval poets are fond of using a rhetorical device known as *occupatio*, where the poet admits his inability to describe. But to remark of one's heroine that one cannot say how beautiful she was is indeed to pay her a compliment worth having. What is more, it is a significant fact about language, whether Chaucer's or ours, that it cannot sufficiently describe everything that we know. When Wordsworth in 'Tintern Abbey' remarks of his younger days

<blockquote>
                         I cannot paint
What then I was . . .,
</blockquote>

he is saying something important about language as well as about himself. The beauty (or ugliness) of ladies, the zest of youth – such matters are indeed indescribable, beyond the broadest terms: you would have to see the lady, or experience or recall youth itself, to know exactly what is meant. Poets who use this figure are drawing attention to one highly underrated fact of language: that it is not capable of doing all the work we have for it to do. They expose a myth fundamental to the subjectivist case, and one I shall call the Omnicompetence of Language.

If language is assumed to be capable of any descriptive task whatever, then the subjectivist view is easier to maintain. But the Omnicompetence of Language is after all an absurd assumption. There are many, many experiences that a given language like twentieth-century English cannot sufficiently describe, and many of them are highly familiar experiences. 'Sufficiently' here means sufficient to distinguish one such experience from any other. Almost everybody, for example, knows with great precision what a banana tastes like, and the evidence for that is that almost everybody can distinguish every instance of banana, and blindfold, from any other taste. So the verb 'to know' is used here in a highly justifiable sense: this is indeed what it is like to know. But nobody can describe that taste sufficiently in words. And this cannot be because our knowledge of that taste is in any way inadequate: the blindfold test disposes of that possibility. It can only be because language itself is inadequate – in this case, in terms for palatal taste. And it is weak in such terms, in all probability, because as a practical matter it can afford to be weak. Anybody who really wants to know what a banana tastes like is in no need of language at all. He can learn it 'ostensively', by eating one.

The Omnicompetence of Language is a considerable oddity, as

myths go. It is odd that literary critics, who are professionally concerned with the limits of language, should need to be reminded that
language has limits. Perhaps they are reluctant to admit a boundary
to their own function: it might smack of self-belittlement. But subjectivists, above all, commonly assume the myth to be a truth, and are
fond of arguing as if you cannot properly be said to know anything
that you cannot describe. They urgently need to have the limits demonstrated to them. What follows from that is of crucial importance in
the domain of critical method. The fact that we cannot describe many
an experience, or individual, or poem, is not a reason for asserting that
we do not know them, or even that we do not know them well. We may
know them with great fullness and accuracy, and yet lack the power to
describe. Knowledge – highly accurate and dependable knowledge,
whether of food or of poetry – can exist independently of an ability to
convey it in words.

Impressions, then, however impressionistic, can be accurate, and
nothing fatal to the objectivity of literary judgements has been demonstrated in showing that such judgements are sometimes or often impressionistic. I wish now to argue something more radical than this:
that there are occasions when accuracy is all the greater for being
imprecise, and in a sense that differs from that in which concepts such
as 'the Sahara' or 'tragedy' can be accurately understood without
being precisely delimited.

★

Many ages of criticism, and none more than the present, are avid for a
general theory of literature. It is hard to see why. A theory that explained the totality of literature, or even some vast area within it such
as tragedy, would plainly diminish its interest. A general theory is
reductive: convenient as it may be, it contracts the object to be studied
in its subtle complexity. Much recent critical theory, from Northrop
Frye to the *Nouvelle Critique*, has failed to take account of this. It is not
just that these grandiose theories have failed to work, at least in the
absolute sense once hoped for them. It is rather that one may be glad
they did fail. It is good to know that the literature of Western man is
not reducible to these fribbles.

Another weakness of critical theory in its grandiose forms is its
claim to be fundamental. It is nothing of the kind. When a general observation is true, its truth is parasitic on the particular instances it

claims to describe. A theory of tragedy depends on knowing tragedies; never, if it is worth a farthing, on anything else. Any generalisation, to be worth anything, needs to represent a summary of particular instances; and any contrary instance weakens or destroys it. Critical theory *cannot* be the foundation of literary knowledge: who ever heard of a foundation that was up in the air? The foundations of literary knowledge are the poems, plays and novels that are there to be known. And what one knows about *Hamlet* or *Phèdre* must always surpass in importance what one knows about the concept of tragedy. The particular takes precedence, and in a double sense: it comes first in the sense that one acquires it first; and it is the stronger of the two. Theory is its slave.

A literary understanding can easily grow deformed if it fails to take account of this. In matters of evidence, one can best look for analogies in courts of law, where the principle is already well understood. A witness who does not claim to understand the total significance of what he saw is more likely to be trustworthy than one who does. And some bad literary criticism is like the testimony of a witness who thinks he understands the affair: 'I saw the whole thing.' Those who believe they understand the whole nature of tragedy or comedy, for just this reason, are likely to be poor readers of tragedies or comedies; just as those who believe that all human history illustrates the hand of God or the class war are unlikely to prove attentive and accurate readers of such social fiction as Dickens or Balzac or Trollope. It is disabling to suppose one knows all the answers before one begins to read. Wordsworth's *Prelude* is the more convincing as autobiography because it abounds with phrases like 'I cannot say . . .' or 'I cannot paint . . .'. Wordsworth *knows* he does not understand the total meaning of his own past life. A critic, in the same way, who remains uncertain about the total significance of works of literature, or less than confident that such meanings can be altogether expressed, need not be charged with prevarication or culpable ignorance. His caution may be well based.

This argument about literary knowledge needs to be pressed further. At the furthest extremes of the question, there are two kinds of knowledge: that which is described or describable in words, and that which is not. In schools of literature the second kind has been gravely underrated, precisely because they are schools. In any highly verbal community such as a classroom, there is a powerful tendency to suppose that any formula is better than the absence of a formula. The critical mind, with its intermittent cravings for abstraction, has rarely excelled at silence. Critics are articulate if they are anything. But silence, or a monosyllable, or a pointed finger, can at times suggest a more advanced state of knowledge than any formula or verbal definition.

Consider the following instance. As a native speaker of English who learned French at school and in travel, I plainly know English better than French. Not just because I speak it more readily and more accurately, but because I can reply with great assurance when asked by a foreigner: 'Can I say this in English? . . .'. I know what is impossible in English as well as what is possible. On the other hand, I know the grammatical rules of French better than those of English, in the sense of being able to state them; and I need to know them better, in that sense, since I cannot speak French without recalling them to mind. For just this reason, I might prove a better teacher of the French language than of English. And yet it seems lunatic to deny that I know English better than French.

A knowledge of rules and definitions, then, is not evidence of relative knowledge but of relative ignorance. True, if I did not know the rules of French grammar, I should know French even less. But then if I were to live in France, and forget them, I might know French even better. A knowledge of the rules is never a symptom of knowledge in the most intimate sense. Those who demand verbal definitions of literary terms like 'tragedy', irony' and 'realism' need to be reminded of this – especially if they claim or assume that to lack definitions is to be ignorant of tragedy or irony or realism. And those who imagine they are capable of defining tragedy are showing their ignorance of tragedies in two ways: their definition is itself ignorant, in that it fails to include all the cases and exclude the rest; and it is also a symptom of ignorance in a more general and damaging sense. No one who had really studied the plays of Aeschylus, Shakespeare, Racine, Ibsen and Pinter beyond the earliest stage would have felt the need for it.

Another instance may count here in a manner at once related and yet distinct. Most of us, most of the time, can tell at a glance the difference between an old man and a young one, and with fair accuracy we can estimate the intermediate stages as well. But few, and with reason, trouble to list the indicators of age: greying and diminishing hair, a stooping figure, a withered skin and the rest. Recognising age, then, though commonly instantaneous, is evidently a perception of some complexity; and no one would want to insist that all the characteristics of age – hair, stoop, skin, and the rest – should be simultaneously present; still less to answer questions about how many are required, or which matters most. There can be no precise answers to those questions that are also true answers; and the more precise, the less true they would be. That will seem a surprising conclusion to those who confuse truth with precision, and the first among many salutary surprises.

On the other hand, it is possible to know about old age in another sense, and one more like that in which an Englishman knows French. A gerontologist knows about age in that way, even to the point of quantifying blood-pressures. Much of the insistence laid upon criticism in recent times, in effect, has been a demand to move from the first kind of knowledge to the second. The sheer prestige of mathematics and the sciences would make that probable. Even a craving for quantification is not unknown in literary studies: it is already partly satisfied in the statistical study of vocabulary. The arts in universities have long felt themselves something of a country mouse, with science as the rich city cousin. The arts cost less, for one thing. They are sometimes in a mood of wishing to cost more, on the principle that what costs more is likely to be more appreciated. They can be bitterly conscious of achieving less than the sciences that is audible and visible. They need no laboratories, only a library. It is natural they should seek at times to pace their rivals, if not outpace them, by entering the same race.

But that race is not for the arts. Those who study literature may need assurance here, but it is an assurance that can reasonably be given. There is a powerful inclination to assume that anything that is not formulaic, like the definitions that govern the terminology of chemistry, or quantifiable, as in statistics, can only be a matter of personal choice. 'Intuition' is the next danger signal in the argument: it is often argued that all subjects are faced with a stark choice of imitating the physical sciences or proceeding intuitively. But what good reason has ever been given for supposing anything of the sort? What grounds are there for assuming that intellectual progress is always of one kind or the other? Distinguishing old men from young, for instance, is plainly neither one nor the other. Most of us do it neither scientifically nor intuitively. And yet we do it efficiently.

Even the arts man's assumption that the physical sciences are necessarily and always exact is a rash assumption. The inspired hunch counts in the laboratory as well as in the library; astronomers are often content to deal in approximate figures in calculating the distances between heavenly bodies; and physicists since Heisenberg have known something called the Uncertainty Principle that governs particles of matter. Our view of the sciences needs enlarging. They do not move assuredly from one established truth to the next, and their history is often one of creative error. 'We cannot identify science with truth', as Karl Popper once remarked,

> for we think that both Newton's and Einstein's theories belong to science; but they cannot both be true, and they may well both be false. ('Conversation with Karl Popper', in *Modern British Philosophy*, ed. B. Magee [1971] p. 78)

A view of the arts may need enlarging, too, if it is thought that the art historian works on a painting, or a critic on a poem, by any process so unitary that it could be summed up by the word 'intuition'. To intuit means to guess more or less justly without evidence, or at least without sufficient evidence. But the critic *has* evidence, after all, and it need not be insufficient. That evidence is the poem itself, and the historical knowledge that interprets it. If he cannot define or quantify it, that is not a reason for denying that his procedure is cognitive – a matter of knowledge. The critic knows literature in a way in which men know what they have experience of. We *know* the ways in which old men look different from young ones, whether we can define those ways or not; and we know them neither by rule nor by intuition, but by experience.

The disagreement of experts, what is more, is often more apparent than real. Eliot and Lewis almost certainly agreed about more aspects of *Paradise Lost* than they could ever have found to disagree about. They emphasised their disagreements, and rightly, because that is how a subject progresses. In a negotiation between statesmen or diplomats, in a similar way, disagreements are rightly given longer attention than those matters where agreement has already been reached or has never been needed. Industrial disputes are much the same. And intellectual disagreements, including those between literary critics, are like negotiations in diplomacy or in the field of labour relations.

But disagreement can be less than real in a subtler sense. Again and again in aesthetic questions and in moral ones, men underrate the extent to which the factual elements in highly complex judgements have shifted the nature of the question itself. They suppose they think differently from their grandparents when the difference is in the nature of the question as well as in the answer given. Sexual morality, for instance, is often said to be more permissive today than half a century ago, and perhaps is; but then factual elements like contraception and family inheritance have shifted the nature of the question itself. If the social arrangements that existed before the First World War could be miraculously reproduced, the case for sexual regulation would look much stronger than it does. When experts disagree or appear to do so, as Johnson and A. C. Bradley disagree about what matters most in Shakespearean tragedy, some of that seeming disagreement can be resolved by considering how different were the questions they supposed themselves to be answering. They had different texts of Shakespeare; they knew radically different performances in the theatre; and above all, Bradley knew the Victorian novel and the questions about human motive it posed, and Johnson did not. Even when taken together, that does not account for all the differences, or even most of them. But it does diminish them.

Again, apparent disagreement can arise when one critic considers one aspect of the object, and another some other aspect; or when they consider different combinations of aspects. Cicero tells a story of a painter who chose five women rather than one as a model of beauty, 'because he did not think everything he needed for beauty could be found in a single body' (*De Inventione*, II 3–4); in the same way, he adds, in writing a handbook on diction 'I did not take up a single model', since no single author exemplifies all the virtues of style. The story makes it easy to imagine a situation in which two painters appeared to disagree about the same model, or two critics about the same poem, when 'disagreement' arose out of a misunderstanding about which element in the case they were considering. Just as one painter might admire the nose while another deplores the chin, so do critics often misinterpret, at an early stage of the argument, the point that is truly at issue between them. Coleridge saw this in the first chapter of the *Biographia Literaria* (1817), when he defended the cognitive status of literature in terms he gratefully recalled from his schoolmaster:

I learnt from him that poetry, even that of the loftiest and seemingly that of the wildest odes, had a logic of its own as severe as that of science; and more difficult, because more subtle, more complex, and dependent on more and more fugitive causes.

More numerous causes, then, to paraphrase Coleridge, and more fleeting, than in most scientific experiments. But none the less 'causes' for that reason, as Coleridge acutely saw. A cause is none the less that because you cannot say what it is, or say it exactly. It would take a poet or critic longer to enumerate the rational considerations that make a poem, often enough, than a scientist to explain his experiment; and what is more, the considerations are more 'fugitive' in much of literature than in much of the sciences: harder to define or delimit. Coleridge's remark about his schooldays is a massive contribution to an understanding of the question, if it is sufficiently pondered. A great poem is often a highly condensed linguistic performance, and the critic may easily despair of unteasing and recounting the whole of its argument. That does not alter the fact that its argument is an argument, or that the critic's account of it is an account, accurate or not. What it does alter is the easy prospect of ever getting to the end of the question – of saying everything that could be usefully or pertinently said. And this helps to explain why criticism rarely finishes with poems. It would be hard to think of a critical essay, however distinguished, that put an end to a question for ever and ever, or even for long. Literary judgements rarely partake of the simplicity that enables them to be totally understood by a great body of individuals; in that respect they are more like moral and political judgements than arithmetical. Johnson's contrast in *Rasselas* is well taken:

> We differ from ourselves just as we differ from each other when we see only part of the question, as in the multifarious relations of politicks and morality. But when we perceive the whole at once, as in numerical computations, all agree in one judgement, and none ever varies his opinion.   (ch. 28)

★

One fashionable way of seeking to discredit the objective status of criticism is to set unrealistically high demands on rationality and description. This process of 'upping the demand' is commonly one of silent assumption, the most vital element in the argument being left unstated. If rationality is silently identified with formal logic, for instance, then it is easy to show that literary criticism is not a rational activity: it does not proceed by the rules of logic books, and never has done. If critical description has to be total in order to qualify as description at all, then it is easy to demonstrate that criticism does not describe works of literature – just as easy as showing that it rarely, if ever, describes the totality of any given work.

But rationality is wider than logic. And description is that even when it omits. Indeed it had better omit. A map of Italy that marked in towns and cities but not villages might be all the more useful for certain purposes than one that included every centre of population. No map includes everything. If it did, as Lewis Carroll once observed, it would be as big as the territory it described; in which case it would indeed be useless. No diagram can afford to include everything: that of the London Underground, for instance, is a description all the more useful for being coded by symbolic colours and for misrepresenting the distances between them for the sake of clarity. A caricature is a kind of description as much as an oil painting or a photo, and can be more telling and informative for some purposes than any formal portrait.

What is more, a misdescription is a kind of description. This needs to be emphasised in any argument about the truth-status of literature and literary criticism. It is sometimes argued, for instance, that a Dickens novel does not describe nineteenth-century England, or that George Orwell's essay 'Charles Dickens' (1940) does not describe his novels, because they can be shown to be wrong. Dickens confuses the facts about the Poor Law, Orwell allegedly mis-states the nature of Dickens's art as a social reporter; and yet Dickens was a great novelist and Orwell a considerable critic. . . . It is easy to conclude here that accuracy cannot count for much in the life of a man of letters. But there are two answers to all that. First, it is in no way obvious that a mistake does not count here, and in the way that mistakes do normally count, against the credibility of the total performance. Dickens and Orwell might have achieved more if they had not committed inaccuracies. And second, a misdescription being a kind of description, its status is not abandoned when it is shown to be inaccurate. On the contrary, it is only because it *is* a description that the question of accuracy or inaccuracy arises at all. That needs to be explained to anyone who supposes that because criticism is often personal, partial and passionate, it follows that it cannot be a description of the poems or paintings it claims to describe. But if it were not that, how could the question of partiality arise? A judge can only be called partial in relation to what he judges. To emphasise the personal elements in criticism is not to weaken the base for the objectivity of literary values, but greatly to strengthen it.

The case of ideology is the most notorious and isolable instance of partiality. It is sometimes suggested that criticism cannot be objective because all critical minds are informed or deformed by ideological presuppositions, or 'theory-laden'. All but that of the critic who makes that very assertion, one might cynically add: the principle of miraculous exemption is often silently invoked by subjectivists at this point. Ideology, to render the whole matter the harder to grasp or to refute, is not always understood here as a doctrine consciously held. Conscious beliefs, like Christianity, liberalism or Marxism, can be readily summarised in their root contentions; and the consequences of those contentions to literary studies can in their turn be recognised and accounted for, or duly discounted. To believe in a Messiah, or in individual liberty as the highest political good, or in human history as class war, along with the considerable baggage of conviction that has traditionally accompanied these familiar assertions, is to identify oneself in a lucid and convenient way. But the matter is less lucid if one is accused, say, of bourgeois or Jewish ideology, especially when these alleged predispositions are supposed to be held unconsciously and inescapably, as a matter of social conditioning or genetic coding. Second-order ideology of this kind, which is a prominent element in Fascist and Marxist criticism, is commonly thought of as beyond argument, which doubtless it is. That is why repression and extermination are natural expedients to such theories.

Ideology of the first order, however, stands in some need of defence in the context of criticism. The first defence is to show that it is not a problem peculiar to literature, or even to the humanities. Genetics, for example, has been wracked by bitter ideological differences; the case of Lysenko, who controlled Soviet biology under Stalin, cannot easily be forgotten. He believed that organisms can pass on the effects of their environmental conditioning to their offspring; and this doctrine, which was plainly intended to shift genetic theory in a Marxist direction from heredity to environment, was enforced by the Soviet state in the 1940s and 1950s. Those who think that the influence of ideology proves that the enquiry is subjective should be compelled to follow their own argument where it goes. If they are right, then genetic science is subjective; and the argument cannot and should not stop there, since genetics is an aspect of medical science that bears on other aspects of medicine. And yet few subjectivists believe that when they consult a doctor about an illness they are entering into a subjective enquiry. They want and expect a cure.

And they do so because the matter is urgently important, and perhaps even a life-and-death matter. This suggests, in its turn, that subjectivism is trivialising as well as philosophically incoherent. It is not the sort of nonsense that anyone allows of a surgeon about to operate or the engineer who designs a bridge one means oneself to cross. But then literary subjectivists plainly do not think literature a life-and-death matter. They think it little better than a game, albeit a highly sophisticated game. As Wordsworth put it in his preface to *Lyrical Ballads*, they 'encourage idleness and unmanly despair':

> It is the language of men who speak of what they do not understand; who talk of poetry as of a matter of amusement and idle pleasure; who will converse with us as gravely about a *taste* for poetry, as they express it, as if it were a thing as indifferent as a taste for rope-dancing, or frontiniac or sherry,

whereas 'its object is truth . . . .'. This is the most fervent point of difference between the opposing schools. An objectivist cannot take literature so lightly. He sees literature as knowledge, and criticism as a way of expounding and diffusing that knowledge. Whether such knowledge is a life-and-death matter must vary according to the historic moment. At all events, it is vital knowledge, and not to be replaced by any other. It is unique. The verb 'to know' would mean little enough if we ceased to observe how much Shakespeare, Goethe and Dickens knew about the human heart.

The second defence is to insist that ideology, in its primary and more familiar sense, is itself an objective enquiry. It is odd that this should need to be said at all. But many an argument about the status of criticism has assumed that ideology is little more than a synonym for prejudice or bias, and rock-ribbed prejudice at that; with the implication that there is no use arguing with that sort of thing, and that people will believe as they do, whether the causes of belief be genetic, environmental, or other. But that assumption is so absurd that it even runs counter to ordinary experience. Everybody, surely, knows, or knows of, someone who has been converted to or from some ideology or other. St Paul on the road to Damascus is one classic instance among millions. It cannot really be true that one cannot argue with ideologies. Many of us argue with them daily, and not always without effect.

To assert that one man in history was the Messiah, or that liberty or the class war play some vital historic role, is surely to make an objective assertion. The Messiah may have been that man, or another, or none, or none so far; and the role of liberty or class may have been conceived or misconceived by such ideologues as Marx or John Stuart Mill. Such assertions can be right or wrong. Granted that they can be shown to be one or the other, when they can, only by exceeding the conventional limits of literary criticism: but then it is hard to imagine anything better for criticism than to exceed those conventional limits. Why should the experts be allowed or encouraged to sit in their little boxes and never listen to anyone in neighbouring departments? Universities are expressly constituted to give opportunities for exchanges between disciplines, and the great critics already have a proud record in giving to others as well as taking from them. William Empson's *Milton's God* (1961), a treatise about God as well as *Paradise Lost*, is an original contribution to theology as well as to English.

Why is critical subjectivism intermittently fashionable? It is so, above all, because it is supposed to confer freedom, especially the freedom of the student from the teacher; so that it flourishes in periods of indiscipline, and wanes in those soberer eras when the young unashamedly seek knowledge. The word 'authoritarian' is of almost inevitable occurrence here. Every subjectivist believes that if he conceded an objective status to critical judgements, he would be waiving his right to think about literature as he pleases. That is why he commonly uses weak arguments and obstinately closes his ears to better ones. He is obstinate in debate because he believes that something precious is about to be filched from him; and he is dogmatic, by a supreme contradiction, even as he claims to believe that conviction is a matter of personal choice. But if that is all conviction is or can be, in moral or aesthetic questions, why is he shouting?

> To think that two and two are four,
>   And neither five nor three,
> The heart of man has long been sore,
>   And long 'tis like to be,

as A. E. Housman once put it. The subjectivist is indeed sore about things being as they are, and independently of his own mind. He is the spoilt child of a literary education, and wants to be allowed to go on believing that poems, plays and novels are whatever he wants them to be.

But freedom to choose is just what objectivism would give him, if only he would listen. Winston Smith, the hero of Orwell's *Nineteen Eighty-Four* (1949), chose freedom at the moment he realised that things are what they are independently of the theories that authority and the Party may spin about them:

> The solid world exists, its laws do not change. Stones are hard, water is wet, objects unsupported fall towards the earth's centre. . . . Freedom is the freedom to say that two plus two make four. If that is granted, all else follows.   (1 7)

All else, one might add, including the conviction that authority can be wrong. This is the truth that makes men free, just as freedom means seeing that there is a truth to be had, if only one were perceptive and persistent enough to have it. Where is the freedom in supposing that anyone's opinion is as good as anyone else's? Lost, in that event, would be the freedom to argue with Tolstoy about Shakespeare, or the freedom to tell a professor, in word or in print, that he is mistaken, and why. In a subjectivist world mistakes are impossible, even inconceivable; and the freedom to tell authority that it is wrong or evil cannot survive that assumption. If truth is not to be found or declared, then neither is falsehood. The subjectivist, if only he could attend carefully to his own arguments and their consequences, is giving up that freedom. No stakes, no winnings, as they say at race-meetings. And what freedom worth having does he get in exchange?

The freedom, it may be answered, to think as he pleases. But if only he knew it, he has that already. Men *are* allowed to think that two and two make three or, like Tolstoy, that Shakespeare was a poor dramatist. It is the great subjectivist dictatorships of fascism and communism that ban liberty of opinion and cherish dogmas about genetic and environmental conditioning, not the objectivist states of the Western world.

And in schools and universities, as in free societies, the modern Tolstoy would still have his chance. A chance means a chance to argue and to produce evidence. If a case like Shakespeare's dramatic poverty is worth making at all, then it is worth making with its supporting arguments. The critical mind is well equipped to judge the cogency of an essay that tries to make that case. It might even carry weight, at least for some of the way. But if critical subjectivism were true, then there would be no weight to be carried. An eccentric or rebellious assertion is only that because of its status *as assertion*. If it is merely a reflection of a view, and in an atmosphere where one view is no more defensible than another, then it remains hopelessly weightless and forever trivial. It tells us about the critic, not about the work.

And the work, with any luck, is more important than the critic. That is why objectivism is more radical and subversive in its consequences than the subjective view of literary judgements, and forever more serious in its purpose.

4 *What History Does*

In the 1930s and 1940s, in the heyday of the Cambridge School and the American New Criticism, literary history was often felt to be moribund, or even dead. Its heir was the new verbal analysis.

The announcement, however, was premature. Since the 1950s literary history has repossessed the field of English studies. The greater part of academic criticism, whether spoken or written, is now conducted within an historical framework. We have lost the old fear of what T. S. Eliot called 'the pastness of the past' – a fear that once bordered on contempt. We no longer believe, as E. M. Forster once claimed as a partial truth in *Aspects of the Novel* (1927), that 'History develops, Art stands still'. But the revival of literary history has been problematical and troubled.

In this chapter I shall consider how and why literary history returned, and in such force; and what its problems and prospects now are.

★

The rejection of history by men of letters and their academic followers in the 1920s and after was based on several considerations. One of these was that it could only be annalistic, in the familiar Victorian way, arranging information rather than discovering it, and necessarily unoriginal. Another was that it was educatively inadequate, even deadening, since it could be memorised at second hand rather than performed individually. And lastly, it was felt to be ultimately unliterary, forever concerned about the causes, circumstances and gossip of literature rather than works themselves.

Since the 1950s, however, these arguments have ceased to look cogent. It is now clear that history, whether literary or other, is under no obligation to be annalistic, or indeed narrative at all. It can itself be analytic. Gibbon and Macaulay wrote narratives, to be sure, but Lewis Namier did not; and yet nobody doubts that Namier in his *Structure of Politics at the Accession of George III* (1929) was writing as an historian. The notion of history itself has widened: it can be about problems as well as periods, as Lord Acton once said it should be; and it can be about a point in time rather than a sequence of events.

And notions have widened in more ways than this. A revived interest in nineteenth-century theories of history, such as the Positivist and the Marxist, have compelled a new interest in the historical spirit itself. One cannot easily revive doctrines of history without reviving historiography. And the relations of literature to other arts and to intellectual progress in general have thrown new prospects open. The study of the English Renaissance, as an example, has been transformed by historians of art and ideas, with philosophy and the visual arts linking literature into new patterns of cultural enquiry. History, it is now clear, had more fields to conquer than the Cambridge School had dreamed of.

As for the anti-educative effects of literary history, it is now easier than it once was to believe the enquiring beginner can be taught how to behave originally and self-reliantly. Historical knowledge need not be secondhand. It is an advancing system that reveals new ignorances wherever it goes. Every solution makes for a new problem, or more than one; and any intelligent beginner can see that this is so. True, an historical enquiry is cumulative, and the beginner is to that extent at a disadvantage; and one reason why practical criticism in its anti-historical mood between the wars attracted enthusiasm was that it was a game anyone could play. It allowed for an ignorance of history, and even in some sense preferred it, since literary history in those days was associated with a set of prefabricated assumptions.

It must be conceded at the outset that the new historical bent of literary studies confers an advantage on experience. All historians profit from a lengthening familiarity with their trade. In many a well-worked field, there is so much to know before one can even estimate what the next step is. Subjects like the causes of the English Civil War are like old coalmines where men walk for hours before reaching the coalface. But it is encouraging here to reflect that there are other subjects where the coalface is near, and some where the coal lies about on the surface, waiting for someone to pick it up. And surface-mining is surely the way to start. Show a student a standard commentary on a poem of Donne or Herbert, for example, and the discussion that follows will rapidly demonstrate which notes are inadequate, and why, and which a future editor might sensibly wish to add. Here is a teaching activity which, conducted as it can be under the generous heading of 'practical criticism', can unite critical, historical, philological and editorial interest. It shows how existing editions are best to be used; and in the very act of showing that, how they might be better than they are. The plain truth is that there are historical problems all around us, easy as well as difficult, all asking to be solved. Not always by beginners: but there are still many the beginner *can* reasonably hope to solve.

The charge that literary history is ultimately unliterary, or at best insufficiently interested in literature for its own sake, is much more fundamental than other objections. It even merits a moment's resentment. Why should literary history be singled out in this way? Political historians are not used to being accused of a lack of interest in politics, or economic historians in economics. Why, then, a literary historian might ask, should he be supposed to have given a working life to literary history unless out of an active interest in literature itself? That answer, and the sense of indignation that naturally accompanies it, may help to clarify the charge that is being made. It is regrettably true that there have been literary historians who were incompetent judges in literary matters, and others whose writings are dry enough to render their interest suspect. But then neither incompetent judgement nor a dry style ever improved literary history; and what is more, there have been 'new' critics as well as historical ones who have been guilty on both counts. The charge cannot justly or reasonably be limited to the literary historian. It is of the nature of intellectual fashion to attract the mediocre, among others. That sort of fashionable inflation in literary history happened between the two 'saints' of its classic era, Sainte-Beuve and Saintsbury. It was a Victorian and Edwardian fashion, and ceased with the First World War; and its revival since the 1950s has been unassuming, untheoretical and without fanfares of trumpets. By now it looks less plausible than ever to suppose that one can compose literary history competently, let alone well, without a highly developed sense of literature itself. To suppose otherwise would require a clinching counter-instance, and it is doubtful if there is one.

Literary history is about the past of literature. Since all literature is from the past, the deep significance of this fact is sometimes over-looked as if it were a truism. But it is a truism that needs to be scanned if sense is to be made of what the historian does. Literary history has its familiar 'stuff': those who pursue it study works in their historical context, busy themselves over relationships with public events and the other arts, edit texts and make bibliographies. They also analyse the great genres such as tragedy and the novel in their ancestral develop-ment, describe coteries and schools, write literary biographies and examine the influences of writer upon writer. More than four-fifths of academic criticism as it is nowadays conducted in books and disserta-tions is comprehended there; probably, too, the greater part of journalistic criticism or reviewing. Newspaper reviewers often inform their readers, and sometimes at length, about the lives of authors and the literary traditions in which they wrote. So do drama critics. Liter-ary history is not a remote activity, then – certainly not only that. It is familiar as well as academic, and millions find it useful as well as seductive. And its use can be explained.

Language is a contextual apparatus, and a message achieves its meaning only by virtue of the circumstances that surround it. This is why, when we receive a letter or a telegram, we normally read the signature first, even though it comes at the end. And it explains how it is that nonsense, which is difficult to achieve in an absolute sense within the limits of a given language, is very easy to achieve within ordinary conversation. A remark is effectively nonsense when no sense can be made of it in its human setting. Since conversation is highly limiting, it is exceptionally easy to achieve nonsense there: literature, being far wider in its conventions, makes the matter much harder. A philosopher recently claimed that certain phrases are irreducibly nonsensical, such as 'participial biped' and 'a man in the key of A flat', as well as that old philosophical favourite 'consanguinity drinks procrastination'; but he was promptly answered by another in the following poem:

> At family reunions
> (Weddings, funerals,
> The joint junketings of Christ and Saturn)
> Blood is so much thinner than whisky and water
> That consanguinity drinks procrastination,
> Postponing the ineluctable anacoluthon
> In the polished Jamesian discourse of Uncle Fred
> (That prosy participial biped)
> When he and Uncle Arthur
> (Literal, inarticulate,
> A man transposed wholly into the key of A flat)
> Discover
> That there are impediments to the marriages of mind
> Certainly more than kin, as certainly less than kind.
> (Hector Monro, 'Nonsense? Nonsense!', *Analysis*, xxx [1973],
> quoting M. C. Beardsley, *Aesthetics* [1958] p. 143)

This little poem, without making poetic claims for itself, contrives to find settings for all three phrases offered in the original challenge, so that all cease to be entirely nonsensical. Meaning is what something means in its context; nonsense is what lacks an intelligible context. Any one of these three phrases would indeed be nonsense in almost any other collocation of words one could devise, whether literary or conversational.

In any highly defined situation, most phrases are nonsensical. On being formally introduced in England, almost any remark except 'How do you do?' would be considered nonsensical. Leigh Hunt's first remark at his first meeting with Coventry Patmore was 'This is a beautiful world, Mr Patmore.' Considered in a certain light, that is a more sensible remark than 'How do you do?', but Patmore understandably concluded that the older man was infinitely eccentric. 'Paris is the capital of France' is far from nonsense, but it would have sounded even worse nonsense at that moment – so much so that Patmore might easily have doubted the sanity of his host.

Literature can usefully be considered as a kind of message, even granting that it is often a shapely message where more considerations than those of making sense reasonably apply. Literature does make sense, after all, even if it does more than that. It is not purely autonomous, or a world of its own. Wordsworth called a poet 'a man speaking to men', which is a salutary reminder; and Samuel Butler is said to have invented the term 'sayee' to represent the reader whom an author needs to imagine if he is to write, and write well. Just as a letter or a telegram presupposes a recipient, or a speech an audience, so does a play suppose a theatrical audience, or a poem or a novel a reader. A certain kind of audience or reader, what is more. If this is a restraint, it is surely a rewarding one. Why else does one make marks on paper and have them printed, unless to be understood? And not just understood by the world at large, but by a reader of a certain kind and in a certain world.

If literature is a message, among other things, then its sense and being are powerfully affected by the context for which it was written: its imagined 'sayee', its allusions, its relation to earlier works, its author's probable intentions – the whole field of historical relations in which it exists. It is a crucial element of some eighteenth-century English fiction that it was written with a readership in view that was chiefly feminine. It is not a minor matter that the opening of *Paradise Lost*, with its invocation to the Holy Spirit as a 'muse', echoes both Homer and Virgil, not to mention the Book of Genesis in Milton's ninth line: 'In the beginning . . .'. That shows that Milton wrote for an audience who would know the *Iliad* and the *Aeneid*, at their best, as well as Scripture; and that in its turn casts a bright light on his expectation of a 'fit audience, though few'. It is an essential fact about Fielding's *Joseph Andrews* that it appeared in 1742, or two years after Richardson's *Pamela*, and that its young hero of beleaguered virtue has a sister called Pamela. The web of imitation and parody that links work to work, or remark to remark in familiar conversation, is a necessary element in comprehension. Remarks exist and take their meaning from the setting provided for them. So do books. And that web of connection is above all what literary history studies; this is what it does.

★

Some of the opportunities and pitfalls of the new literary history may now be considered. Since it is a kind of history, some of these considerations will run wider and deeper than literature, and concern the writing of history in general.

1. *False evidence may be significant as well as true.* It is a misunderstanding to suppose that good evidence is the same as true, for the historian, or bad the same as false. Detection provides an illustration here. Agatha Christie once wrote a crime novel called *Murder on the Orient Express* where, to simplify the plot, a murder was committed in which all the suspects were guilty. All the suspects, as was natural, lied; but the detective, after questioning them in turn, discovered the truth. What is more, he knew or suspected that they were all lying. But if he had attended only to evidence he knew to be true, he could not have solved the case. It was the lies, and above all the relations between the lies, that gave him the right answer.

A lie is only one kind of false evidence, and the simplest. There are ignorances, whether innocent or wilful, on the part of witnesses; conscious and unconscious suppression; and slips of tongue and pen. As a practical matter, the historian cannot avoid false evidence. He is in no position to insist on the true and on nothing but. Indeed, there is no such thing, in all probability, as a reliable body of evidence, and political historians who mock at the notion of using novels as evidence for what happened in history need to be reminded of this. To that extent all historians have to behave like Agatha Christie's detective. Parish records are fallible and omissive, newspapers distort, and the very texts of literary documents are often problematical, especially when they are medieval or early modern. It is just as well that false evidence counts as well as true. Sometimes it is all there is.

2. *Silence is significant as well as evidence.* 'The dog did not bark in the night,' Sherlock Holmes pregnantly remarked, solving the case of the hound of the Baskervilles. The mark of the true historian is to hear significance in the sound of nothing. It is profoundly significant, and not only in the study of Shakespeare, that his plays reveal no certain knowledge of Greek tragedy; that Corneille's and Racine's reveal none of Elizabethan drama; or that Dickens, especially in his early fiction, so rarely reports the mental life of his characters from within. The reasons why these things are so, and their consequences, and their partial or possible exceptions, are questions to stretch the mind and extend debate.

3. *Much history is based on assumptions,* and some of them may be merely habitual. Habitual assumption is the supreme conservative

force in any enquiry; and its chief weapon is terminology, which can preserve assumptions in debate even when the evidence is weak or null. It is always easy to assume that a name is a name for something, in the sense of something that exists or once existed. If people talk about a 'bourgeoisie' for long enough, it can become a strenuously difficult matter to persuade the world that no sufficient evidence has ever been offered to prove there ever was such a thing. The radical mind can feel lonely at such moments. But the scientific analogy of phlogiston may cheer him up. Phlogiston was accepted by eighteenth-century chemists as a name for the combustible element in objects that are capable of burning – until Lavoisier, late in the century, proved that it did not exist at all.

There is a good deal of phlogiston in the study of literature. What is the evidence for thinking the eighteenth century an Age of Reason; or for supposing that neoclassicism was ever any kind of classicism; or for believing that a working or middle class ever existed in England – let alone a 'working-class literature' or a 'bourgeois culture'? That many have been convinced of these things is some sort of a beginning to the argument, but it is nothing like enough. They could have been wrong. That is why the critical sense needs to be resolutely hostile to terminology. Terms conserve assumptions: criticism questions, attacks, demands, and demands again, that more (and more sufficient) evidence be produced. At its best it is unsatisfied with easy excuses, unimpressed by fashion, and unappeased by cunning silence. It is tenacious and outspoken. It is the small boy who cries out that the emperor has no clothes.

4. *Men often believe in incompatibles*, often because they do not follow where their own arguments lead. Some educationists, for example, believe both that teaching should be less authoritarian *and* that interdisciplinary studies should be encouraged. But interdisciplinary studies, whatever their virtues, always tend to be authoritarian. To study a single subject is to make oneself free with it, to the point of questioning the teachers and challenging the experts. But to study the relations between subjects can only mean to accept the word of experts, each in his own field; and that acceptance is authoritarian.

The instance illustrates how incompatibles can coexist when there is a vested interest in keeping them from collision. Everybody is tempted to protect his own preferences and prejudices from the cold wind of analytical debate. And it would be a rare being who never contradicted himself. Milton believed that the ways of God to man

could be justified; he also thought them to be such that even the elo-
quence of Milton could barely justify them. Yeats believed both in the
leadership of an Anglo-Irish aristocracy in Ireland, and in a political
independence that would confer power on a hostile majority. Bertrand Russell, so Keynes once argued,

> sustained simultaneously a pair of opinions ludicrously incom-
> patible. He held that in fact human affairs were carried on after a
> most irrational fashion, but that the remedy was quite simple and
> easy, since all we had to do was to carry them on rationally. (J. M.
> Keynes, *Two Memoirs* [1949] p. 102)

It is always risky, then, to say of an author that he could not have
believed x since he believed y, and on no ground but that x and y are
incompatible.

5. *Some coincidences in the evidence are genuinely that.* They can be fortu-
itous, and there is always a danger of 'seeing pictures in the fire' and
supposing them significant.

The difficulty here is one of assessing probabilities. How do we
know, or rightly suspect, that resemblances within a work as large as
Spenser's *Faerie Queene* or Dickens's *Bleak House* are significant, or in
what sense they are so? How do we estimate the interest of similarities
between the dark lady of Shakespeare's sonnets and an historical
person of the 1590s? Mathematicians, it is said, can provide a formula
to 'explain' any random series of numbers whatsoever. But the figures
were none the less set down at random; and literary historians can
easily grow as over-ingenious as mathematicians. Some, like the
patient gamblers in casinos who copy the numbers that come up in
roulette in the hope of finding a pattern, are inadequately versed in
the theory of probability. It may, after all, be pure coincidence that
Spenser's 'Epithalamion' has 365 long lines, and the figure need not
represent the days of the year; even though it is granted that nume-
rology, or an interest in the mystic significance of numbers, was a
concern of some Renaissance thinkers. Some external evidence, like
a remark of Spenser's or of a contemporary, would be needed to
make any such significance a probability here.

6. *When a theory fails on the evidence, it is often better to scrap it than to mend
it.* The archaeological zeal of historians, including literary historians,
can be excessive. The present age is engagingly dedicated to intellectual revivals: the Enlightenment, Positivism and Marxism have all

found recent disciples, though they are all well over a century old and lack any clearly continuous existence as systems of belief. *Ut pictura, poesis* – the classical and Renaissance doctrine of a parallel between poetry and painting has its modern partisans among iconographers, and somebody may even attempt some day to revive the doctrine of the dramatic unities of time, place and action. The market for historical revival being what it is, it is doubtful if any limit can be put to the convictions that intelligent men are prepared on occasion to entertain or even to endorse.

Conviction can be of varying kinds and varying intensity, and some of the partisanship in question here may border on innocent affectation. But it is still clear that many of the intellectual revivals promoted by the new literary history mould the convictions of those who attend to them. There is an element of irresponsibility, then, in reviving dogmas in a manner that pays no heed to their truth-content. To dig up the intellectual past is, in the end, to engage in persuasion; and we need to ask, sometimes clamorously, what we are being invited to believe. Revivals of Renaissance Platonism and nineteenth-century Marxism are disquieting instances of the historian's power. Sometimes they are discussed in a rhetoric neither committed nor uncommitted, neither credulous nor incredulous; they are entertained for the sake of intellectual titillation. Their historical interest is real; but somebody should dare to say that their highest interest lies in the proof they offer that intelligent men can sometimes believe in foolish things. The historian does not have to behave like the Irish judge who is reported to have swerved neither to partiality on the one hand nor to impartiality on the other. He should prefer truth to falsehood and say so. It matters, in the end, whether what an author has written is persuasive or not.

★

History is a form of power. That is a warning, not a boast. 'He who controls the past controls the future,' as the rulers of Orwell's *Nineteen Eighty-Four* knew. No wonder literary history has returned to such active life. It is the way by which power is exercised over reputation, and power is not easily neglected, or for long. What men see in the debates of past ages can form their convictions all too easily, on occasion, and all too permanently. That is why the root problem of literary history is not that it should have too little influence, but that it should so easily have too much. It is a power of mind, and a limit will somehow have to be found to it. If Hegel and Marx can be revived as intellectual influences in the later twentieth century, so can Carlyle and the progenitors of fascism. Stranger things have already happened. It is to the critical and questioning spirit alone that is confided the momentous task of braking and confining the abundant energies of the historical temper. Criticism can control history, though it does not always succeed in doing so as well as it should. But it is hard to see that there is anything else that can.

5 *Language or Linguistics*

To see a word for the first time either as substantive or adjective,
in a connection where we care about knowing its complete meaning, is the way to vivify its meaning in our recollection.

George Eliot

We all know about language, because we all use language. No
similar conclusion is drawn from the fact that we all use kidneys,
nerves and intestines.

Anthony Burgess

Linguistics is the science of language. And literature is composed of
language. It looks natural, then, to call linguistics to the help of criticism.

But that call, though often made, has not been convincingly
answered by linguistics in the years since 1945. Critics have been left
to do their unaided best with literary language; some study of such
language has, after all, been an element in practical criticism since the
1920s. But co-operation with linguists has remained fitful and largely
fruitless.

In this chapter I shall consider why linguistics has contributed so
little to literary studies in the past generation, and what critics can do
about it.

Linguistics has undergone two sweeping revolutions in the past century, along with innumerable shifts of position. The problem in co-
operation lies just here. Its inclination towards continuous change –
in terminology if not in substance – has often been a prime difficulty in
attempts to collaborate.

The first revolution, initiated by Ferdinand de Saussure in his Geneva lectures of 1906–11, *Cours de linguistique générale* (1916), attacked the 'diachronic' or historical study of language that had dominated the subject in the nineteenth century, with its interest in historical grammar along with normal or 'correct' usage. Saussurian linguistics, by contrast, claimed to be severely descriptive. The difference can be most simply expressed in terms of intellectual models. Just as Victorian philology had imitated history, so did pre–1914 structuralism imitate science: a view of science, what is more, commoner at the turn of the century than it is today – scrupulously non-evaluative in its quest for objectivity, and dogmatically convinced that value-judgements are personal and non-scientific.

It was after Saussure, or in the decades between the wars, that the professional study of language was transformed. It veered away from the historical concerns of philology, of which the *Oxford English Dictionary* is the greatest monument in the English language, towards linguistics, which aspired to describe a given language at a given point in time, or 'synchronically'. In the years after the Second World War the influence of structural linguistics was to run outwards into sociology, anthropology, literary criticism and other humanities.

The second revolution began with Noam Chomsky's *Syntactical Structures* (1957), which revived interest in what had once looked a discredited concern with grammar and inherited systems of rules. Chomsky's case was based on the mystery of aptitude. How is it that infants learn their mother tongue to perfection, and in so few years, and by example only – unless the human mind is constituted at birth to receive certain patterns of language? Nature must play its part as well as nurture, and it may not have been absurd of the European Renaissance to have interested itself in Latin grammar, or even the prospect of a universal grammar underlying all human language. The ideal of the correct in speech suddenly looked less absurd. So far as the relation between literary and linguistic studies was concerned, the chief effect of Chomsky was to destroy the dominance of structuralism and to encourage a renewed tolerance of historical grammar. And in doing that it opened the prospect of a new interest in literature among professional linguists. If they had followed that argument where it led, they might even have come to accept that rules and judgements are not merely personal and subjective; that they are an essential aspect of language; and that the exercise of critical judgement deserves some tolerance too, and some respect. The ultimate hope of the Chomskyan phase of linguistics in the 1960s was that linguists might abandon their disinclination to analyse literary language, which structuralists before them had commonly dismissed as exceptional. A prospect of co-operation between criticism and the professional study of language opened; and some critics, though few enough linguists, worked to make it happen.

The collapse of structuralism in the 1960s is an instructive event. Its claim had been to total description. It aspired to describe a given language, always common rather than literary, in a given era, which was usually the present; and literature was invited to wait until it had succeeded. It never succeeded. No such description was ever achieved as a totality, and structuralism now looks like a fascinating mirage of the early twentieth-century mind. Desert travellers report that they can tell a mirage by the gap between itself and the earth below. That gap was visibly there in structuralism. There was never any reason to suppose that any language is a structure existing out of time. A language comes from somewhere, and its origins are an element in what it means and how it works. Words and phrases often bear their family trees about with them: some famous instance of their use, perhaps, as in a comedian's catch-phrase, or a regional or dialectal flavour, or an element of irony or parody that demands a recollection of something outside itself – the something, whatever it is, that is being ironised or parodied. We quote words as well as use them, and there is an ultimate sense in which all the language that we use is a remote species of quotation or misquotation. Some people, wittingly or unwittingly, even quote themselves, like Nym in Shakespeare's *Henry V* with his 'That's the humour of it'. The proverb, which is common to all native speakers of a language, is an exceptionally simple instance of this principle. That is why a language cannot be abstracted out of history without abstracting it altogether. It lives, like an old lady surrounded by her possessions, in the unbroken memory of its own past.

But the failure of structuralism was costly. For about half a century it diverted the attention of linguists away from literary language, and inevitably so. The most striking external difference between Victorian philology and twentieth-century linguistics lies just here: the philologists had been obsessed with literature, as the vast armoury of literary quotation in the *Oxford English Dictionary* shows; the linguists, by contrast, disdained literary evidence as aberrant, and analysed popular speech. There was never more than the faintest hope of an effective collaboration between structural linguistics and criticism. Critics may rejoice, then, in the death of structuralism, as of a philistine enemy. But they can take little pride in having helped to kill it. It was killed in a palace revolution that took place within linguistics itself. And the cost of so much fruitless expenditure of energy over half a century must now be counted. English still has no historical grammar that takes account of recent discoveries in the field, and its vast literary heritage is still only scantily described in terms of language. The *OED*, which began to appear as the *New English Dictionary* in 1888, continues to breed supplements, but individual authors remain ill provided. There is no full lexicon of Chaucer's works to gloss the whole of his vocabulary, with its derivations; and none of Shakespeare's since C. T. Onions, *A Shakespeare Glossary* (1911, revised 1953). Etymology, or the science of word derivation, was frowned on by structuralists, as they frowned on all historical enquiry. Modern linguists have still contributed little or nothing to areas of vital concern to literary historians: the evolving use of critical terms since Dryden, for instance, or of terms of social debate such as 'class' or 'culture' since 1800. In all such enquiries structural linguistics, self-immured in its own procedural superstitions, was incapable of helping or of trying to help. It obstinately held that linguistics, being descriptive, must never make judgements of value; that literary criticism, for this reason, was not an objective enquiry and provided no partner in collaboration; that literature, being individual and deviant, is of less concern to the linguist than ordinary speech; and that the past must wait till the present has been provided for.

The Chomskyan phase of linguistics in the 1960s, being more hospitable to a study of the past and interested in the regulative principles of language, promised something better as a collaborative idea. But it must be confessed that its promise, as seen from the standpoint of the literary historian, has largely proved unfulfilled. It remains a conceivable possibility, but hardly a fact. One can imagine a Chomskyan analysis of a poem by Shakespeare, say, or Donne, that would analyse its grammatical base in an historical context, demonstrating how that base differed from that of comparable poems in other languages – source-poems, perhaps – such as the Latin of Ovid or Catullus. But to say that is to indicate how plain it is that the tasks of criticism must be performed by critics. They may be critics trained in linguistics, and to their profit. But they cannot reasonably hope to delegate the study of literature to professional linguists. The linguists themselves do not accept that responsibility, and for good reason. Their training is otherwise. Literature remains in their judgement a minor and deviant sub-species of language, to be approached with caution: a data-bank which, precisely because of its highly personal oddities, must remain of limited illustrative use.

Nor can critics realistically suppose that linguistics will ever present them with a master key to literature. There is always, notoriously, a Master-Key Myth abroad in schools of literature: in the early 1960s it was sociology, which was replaced by anthropology, which in its turn was replaced by linguistics. But no key will turn all the locks of human knowledge. None will reveal the whole of literature, certainly, if only because literature is itself enormously heterogeneous. And there are reasons more specific than this why the contribution of language study to literature, though real, must remain a limited one.

★

First, the units in which linguists have worked in this century have been small, and it is doubtful if they are growing much larger. The phonetician has studied sounds, the lexicographer words, and the analysis conducted by structuralists and Chomskyites was commonly limited to the single sentence at the most. A sonnet looks small to a literary historian. But to a linguist it can look an object too vast for study, though Roman Jakobson has attempted it as an heroic feat in *Shakespeare's Verbal Art in 'Th' Expence of Spirit'* (1970) with L. G. Jones; and a novel, even the shortest, is commonly felt to be out of range altogether.

Second, most schools of linguistics are terminology-bound. An uncharitable observer might be tempted to say that much modern linguistics is devoted to inventing new and more polysyllabic ways of saying something an older school was efficiently saying in fewer and shorter words. The four-letter simplicity of 'noun' and 'verb' does not recommend itself to the professional mind yearning for ever sharper and more descriptive tools. An intelligent critic, by contrast, is not looking for new ways of saying something he can say already – especially not if the new way is less lucid than the old. He is looking for something he does not yet know, or does not yet know how to describe; and he turns to linguistics, if at all, in the hope of discovering more about the language of literature. He seeks tools that are indispensable to the act of discovery. That amounts to a vital and continuing difference of attitude and function. It is the difference between a technical discipline that thinks itself under no obligation to make its findings available to the general reader, on the one hand, and a widely educative activity on the other. .

Third, almost all linguists have seen literary style as a deviation from the ordinary. And not only linguists: this fiction is often accepted readily enough by men of letters, and is probably of their invention. 'In the beginning was the word,' as many believe, and the spoken word at that – forgetting that literature influences speech as well as speech literature. It is significant that linguists take the priority of speech for granted rather than proclaim it: that suggests how much the fallacy is part of the cultural air we breathe. Style, as Paul Valéry once remarked, is a deviation from a norm. The effect of this fallacy upon linguistics has been to offer it an easy pretext for not talking about literature at all, or at least not yet.

But it *is* a fallacy, after all, if 'ordinary' means what happens in conversation and 'literary' what occurs in poems, plays and novels. Style can easily be an element of conversation as well as of books. Conversation, too, can deviate from a norm. If Dylan Thomas's friends are to be believed, his speech was no more commonplace than his writings; and Henry James in his last years was famous for talking like a book, especially one of his own. Some plays and novels, on the other hand, like Harold Pinter's *Caretaker* or Angus Wilson's *Anglo-Saxon Attitudes*, come well within hailing distance of what is recognisable in life around us. Great conversationalists often use words and phrases unexpectedly; and many people, including uneducated people, employ literary arts when they tell anecdotes. There is no total difference between ordinary language and the language of literature, and the reluctance of linguists to consider literature is based upon a misapprehension.

And finally, the terminologies into which linguists of various schools have bound themselves earnestly aspire to the rigour of verbal definition. In this sense linguistics often looks quaintly positivistic to the advanced literary mind. In circles where linguists gather, it is often thought a fatal objection to using terms like 'morpheme' or 'phoneme' if they can be shown to be indefinable. The next move in the game is to invent a new term equipped with a definition which, in its turn, is supposed to work better. Since much of the terminology of literary criticism is indefinable, all this looks weirdly superstitious to the literary critic. He is conscious, as he needs to be, that one can know what a word means, and know it well, without being able to define it. Many words are indefinable by a single and sufficient formula, as any dictionary will show. The use of the word 'mind' in this paragraph, in one of the twenty-one senses listed in the *OED*, illustrates this principle. (It occurs there as sense 17h.)

All this leads to a body of conclusions that can be quickly summarised. Critics cannot dispense with a study of language; but they cannot reasonably hope that linguistics, as it is now constituted, can tell them much about literary language. The linguist is not even looking at literature, for most of the time. And when he does, he rarely sees anything the critic can use. Linguistics as it now exists is not an aid to criticism, and linguists are the first to say so. In higher education, as a matter of ordinary observation, it is an alternative to the study of literary language rather than an auxiliary.

It is because criticism has not always seen this, or wanted to see it, that it has wasted time in seeking collaboration. The choice before the critic today, in bold terms, is language or linguistics. Odd as that proposition must look, it can be justified within the existing system. And far from being resented in linguistic circles, it is certain to be greeted with relief. With the rarest exceptions, linguists today do not want to be bothered with literary language or with those who study it.

★

How, then, should a critic look at language?

The first essential is that he should indeed look at language in its instances, rather than at a theory of language. Theory is parasitic: if it does its work at all, it can only summarise what the individual instances tell. Much of the recent literary enthusiasm for linguistics is based on the secret hope of a universal law, and there are those proclaiming an interest in linguistics who cannot tell a noun from a verb and who look bored when shown how.

A study of literary language should at least guarantee this: that the actual instance – the poem – is sovereign; and that theory, if it is worth anything, should serve an analytical end. Literature has the enormous advantage of existing already. A literary masterpiece is already a fact beyond imagining, in the sense that if it did not exist we should be incapable of imagining it. It is a wonder it should be there at all; and it is that sense of wonder that tempts the supreme tribute of analysis. How did it happen? And how was it done? A poem is already more than any theory could ever be, and it cannot be allowed to sink for long into the status of mere illustration. It is one of the lasting strengths of practical criticism as a tool of study that the poem remains from first to last the object in view.

We can now take stock of what occurred in the Saussurian revolution. When linguistics replaced philology in English-speaking countries in the years between the wars, it wilfully demolished one of the larger achievements of the Victorian historical genius. What English now needs is a revival of philology in the context of literary study. That is in no way impossible to achieve. Philology has never died. Over half a century it has suffered a loss of status, a lack of activity and a famine of funds. And yet in its heyday, in the decades before the First World War, it provided something more than a prospect of co-operation between language and literature. It provided the thing itself.

Philology, as the word has been used in English since the eighteenth century, has come to mean something more usefully confined than its original sense of a love of literary learning. For more than two hundred years in England it has meant the documentary study of language: classical, Hebrew and Sanskrit, and by the nineteenth century the modern vernaculars such as English. When it came to be applied to the new academic study of the national language in Victorian times, it produced editions of medieval texts like those of the Early English Text Society; studies in historical grammar and vocabulary like those of the Society for Pure English; and historical lexicography. Its greatest monument in English is the *Oxford English Dictionary*, which lists English words since 1150, analysed historically by literary quotation.

The literary advantages of philology over linguistics are solid. Whenever a literary historian uses the *OED*, as William Empson used it as the foundation of his critical masterpiece *The Structure of Complex Words* (1951), its advantages are there to be seen. Philology possesses a bank of useful terms, and especially terms of grammar, syntax and metre, that are widely understood outside the confined world of the language expert: terms like sentence, clause and phrase; simple, compound and periodic sentences; names for parts of speech such as noun, verb and adjective; for the functions of verbs, such as active and passive, indicative and subjunctive, and tenses such as past, present and future; and for the common metrical forms. Linguistics has tended to depreciate many of these terms in the present century, on the grounds that they are insufficiently precise or descriptive. But it has rarely succeeded in establishing new terms in their place. What it has done is to create outside its own professional field a chaos of declining confidence, and the educational effects of that chaos have been marked. Many who study literature have been made to feel over the past decades that they should wait till an acceptable terminology has been agreed among experts. And the effect of waiting has been to sap confidence in any sort of teaching or learning of syntax or metre. The study of language, like the Chinese empire in more than one age of its history, has been laid waste by living through a period of permanent revolution.

All this makes the new prospect of a revived philology the more inviting. There are discoveries to be made, and even easily made, by anyone who attends to the elements of language for long enough to acquire a working knowledge. In *The Structure of Complex Words*, which deserves more imitations than it has yet received, Empson showed how near the surface much of the evidence lies. To sift and interpret that evidence, needless to say, will call for persistence and acuity; but as evidence it is abundant, neglected and fertile in opportunities.

★

Consider the English pronoun in the second person. English is the only great European language to have abandoned the *you/thou* distinction, a change that occurred in literary English in the course of the seventeenth century for reasons still largely unclear. It was originally a distinction of rank, as between master and servant, and seems to have been in a state of dilapidation by the later Middle Ages. Malory's Lancelot and Guinevere, as the very types of courtly love, address each other formally as 'you' on all occasions but one. Shakespeare addresses the youth in the sonnets sometimes as 'thou' and sometimes as 'you', and the mistress sometimes in the third person, but his use of these forms has never been conclusively explained. Why do Rosalind and Celia, though apparently equal in rank as cousins, and the best of friends, address each other unequally in the second scene of *As You Like It*? And why does Lear, when he divides his kingdom (I i), address Goneril and Regan as 'thou' and his beloved Cordelia as 'you'?

Or consider the tenses of the English verb. It is an illusion to suppose that the past tense chiefly serves in literature to signalise events in the past. The historic present, after all, can well do that, as Carlyle's *French Revolution* (1837) abundantly illustrates. The past is the commonest tense in the English novel even when, as in Jane Austen, events are supposed to occur in the present age, and even though we know that in strict truth they have never occurred at all.

That tense predominates in fiction because it is the traditional tense of narration. It conventionally announces that a story is being told rather than an exposition attempted. This explains why conversational anecdotes, even when they are about imaginary events, are commonly in the past tense. And yet the tense of the verb has rarely been studied in English fiction except in strikingly exceptional instances like Dickens's *Bleak House*, where the contrasting tenses of past and historic present are used in bold and arresting alternation. It has been studied even less in English poems: Donne's *Songs and Sonets* would provide an interesting ground; or Wordsworth's eight-line elegy, if it is that, 'A Slumber Did My Spirit Seal', where the tense changes in mid-point for a reason worthy of some consideration.

Vocabulary is another neglected area. Most of the great English poets are now provided with concordances; and since that tedious process can now be delegated to a computer, more of them are likely to follow. A concordance to Shakespeare, whether the old Bartlett or the new Harvard, is an essential tool in English studies, and not only for the study of Shakespeare. Where doubts arise about the sense of a word in any other Renaissance author, such as Marlowe, Bacon, Hooker or Donne, one question that plainly needs to be answered can be quickly answered: how did Shakespeare use that word, if he did?

The problem with prose is naturally more intractable: the Columbia edition of Milton has an index (1940) that covers his prose as well as his verse; but no English novelist is provided for in this way, and it is perhaps too much to hope that they could be. R. W. Chapman's edition of Jane Austen (1923–54), however, includes appendices on her vocabulary, grammar, modes of address, punctuation and literary allusions. Voluminous novelists like Dickens or Henry James can still be analysed in samples, provided that questions concerning their use of language are precisely framed and provided that some firm sense of linguistic history is maintained. The first paragraphs of novels are perhaps the most inviting of all; and just because they stand first they can be excerpted with slight loss to context and rewardingly analysed in terms of syntax and vocabulary.

Parts of speech are of greatly underrated interest in literary analysis. Shakespeare, who provides a vast mine of almost all the rhetorical devices known to English, offers instances of deliberate confusions or smudging of function here: nouns can be used for verbs, as in 'He words me' or 'Uncle me no uncle'; and the present participle, a part of speech intermediate between noun and verb, can be turned to special effect. When Macbeth speaks grimly of 'the deep damnation of his taking off' (i vii 20), the smudging provides him with an apt euphemism for Duncan's murder. These artistic uncertainties grow richer in twentieth-century verse, or at least more abundant. Dylan Thomas's 'Fern Hill' abounds in teasing uncertainties of this sort: in the line 'Down the rivers of the windfall light', is 'light' a noun or an adjective? And how does the present participle succeed in dominating so much of the poem, and to what purpose?

Syntax, or the shape of the sentence, is of neglected literary interest, and its relation to metre is especially inviting. The opening stanzas of Gray's 'Elegy Written in a Country Churchyard' may look syntactically simple, perhaps because they are so familiar. But is it so common to use the verb 'to toll' transitively, and in an inversion that suggests that the sound tolls the sense? If the metaphor is that the 'parting day' tolls a curfew, bidding all turn home, then the syntactical inversion – a sort of elegant and teasing confusion of syntax – can be studied through the poem:

> The ploughman homeward plods his weary way,
> And leaves the world to darkness and to me.

Why are 'weary', and 'darkness and . . . me', so placed here? And in

> And all the air a solemn stillness holds

which is the subject and which the object of the verb? And do these syntactical confusions accumulate throughout the poem, or stop? And to what purpose?

★

A revival of philology within literary studies is now overdue. But Victorian as philology once was, it will not look Victorian in its new life. It will set questions the nineteenth century hardly dreamed of. But it can still rejoice in a continuous tradition. There have always been individual scholars, notably editors and lexicographers, who have shown spirit enough not to abandon it, though their spirit does not easily bring them out of their libraries into the wilder worlds of active critical debate or classroom teaching.

But a wider awareness of language in its historical framework, from Old English to Middle English to modern, would have effects on literary study that were both instant and desirable; and it could perform usefully with little if any terminology beyond the most familiar. It would put some backbone into practical criticism, which can easily degenerate into opinionated rambling. It would draw critical essays closer to the texts they claim to describe. And it could provide a solution to the deep-felt hunger among students of literature for a common fund of skill and knowledge to be shared and advanced.

What is more, a new philology could even provide a practical link between the study of literature and the place of English as a world language. To have studied Shakespeare, Milton, Wordsworth and Dickens for what their language has to reveal is indeed to have studied them: a far matter from the empty bombinations that sometimes pass for critical utterance. And it could define and sharpen a consciousness of the mother tongue, as it is spoken and written in the present age, and show how best to teach it to others.

Part Two
The Tools of the Trade

What is now proved was once only imagined.

William Blake

Man only plays when, in the full meaning of the word, he is a man; and he is only completely a man when he plays.

Friedrich Schiller

6   *How to Read:*
or Practical Criticism

If you have built castles in the air, your work need not be lost;
that is where they should be. Now put the foundations under
them.

Henry David Thoreau

When you are at school and learn grammar, grammar is very
exciting. I really do not know that anything has ever been more
exciting than diagraming sentences.

Gertrude Stein

Practical criticism is a training in reading. Its object is to learn to read
literature as an expert.

When an expert studies a work of art, he perceives it not only as a
finished object but as the end of a process. The art historian sees not
just a face or a landscape, but the brushwork that has made that face
or landscape. The critic, in the same way, sees in some measure how
the poem came to be written, and how it might have been written
otherwise. That is why poets are themselves often practical critics.
Wordsworth's 'infirmity', as he modestly described in a letter written
as an old man, was of this sort:

I have employed scores of hours during the course of my life in
retouching favourite passages of favourite authors, of which labour
not a trace remains, nor ought to remain. (18 January 1840)

Johnson's examination of Pope's epitaphs, at the end of his life of Pope
in *Lives of the Poets* (1779–81), is inescapably criticism by one who is
himself a poet; so is Keats's remark about how Shakespeare must

have written some of his sonnets, in a letter of November 1817: 'They seem to be full of fine things said unintentionally – in the intensity of working out conceits.' The first expert, after all, is the artist himself.

The poet knows how the poem was made, because he made it. If candour and memory serve, he can reconstruct much of the creative process: why one metre was chosen rather than another, what difficulties and compromises it gave rise to as he wrote, and in what mood of satisfaction or discontent the poem was finished. And he knows, as anyone who has ever written a poem knows, that poems are not so much finished as abandoned. The hardest decision an artist has to take is to relinquish a process of revision which could in principle be unending. Experience, as a great conductor once remarked, is knowing what to accept.

Knowing how a work was made means seeing it not as a stroke of fortune but as the end of a process, and often of a long one. Artists see their own works in that way, and that is why the ideal practical critic would be the poet himself – assuming only that he is willing to reveal what he knows and is articulate enough in critical prose to reveal it. Carlyle in his *Reminiscences* (1881) complained how Wordsworth only wanted to talk about 'the mechanical part' of poetry, including the etymologies of words, remaining 'stone *dumb* as to the deeper rules, and wells of Eternal Truth and Harmony', and speaking only 'as a wise tradesman would of his tools and workshop'. Amateurs of poetry, like Carlyle, often see poems as fortunate visitations. They admire what they imagine to be an act of spontaneity; they are bored by technicalities, and surprised to learn that creation means muscle and sweat. Blake is said to have remarked, on seeing one of Constable's sketches: 'Why, this is not drawing, but inspiration'; to which Constable remarked quietly: 'I never knew it before; I meant it for drawing.'

Practical criticism differs, then, from ordinary reading. It is meant to differ. There would be slight reason for teachers to teach or students to study something they already know and do by nature. Any profession does things an amateur cannot do: that is the mark of its professionalism. But practical criticism does not threaten ordinary reading, any more than Blake's enthusiasm for pictures was killed by Constable's more professional comment. The ordinary and the professional coexist, sometimes in the same individual. Blake was a professional artist as well as a poet, though one would not guess that from his remark. If they had been looking at a poem of Blake's, Constable might well have called it inspiration, and might not have been wrong. The amateur has every right to his enthusiasm. He is the great public of the arts. But the critic, who began as that, is something more as well.

The superstitious horror that practical criticism provokes in some quarters is surely misplaced. Some of it is a mere 'terror of the cognitive': a fear that knowledge desiccates, that all scholarship is dry as dust, and that only enthusiasm counts. Anyone who supposes that must be ignorant, and perhaps wilfully ignorant, of scholarship itself in its range and depth: it can awaken as well as deaden, open dead tombs of forgotten knowledge, and present to the life of mind more worlds to love. And to love, after all, is itself an act of knowledge.

But hostility can be based on something more specific than this: a horror of analysis. 'Why break a butterfly upon a wheel?' The amateur is characteristically reverent of works of art; and his reverence, however engaging, must in the end be marked down as a sign of ignorance. He hesitates fearfully to run his finger across the surface of an oil painting or to dismantle a poem like a mechanic stripping an engine. He is afraid of breaking something. And still more, he can be afraid of loving literature less when he discovers what makes it work, and may need to be persuaded what a tough thing a poem is. It can be fed in and out of machines for concordances, analysed by linguists for its vocabulary or grammatical properties, and pillaged by historians of language for philological evidence. But there it remains, *aere perennius*, as Horace put it: more lasting than bronze. Practical criticism never did any poem lasting harm. Or any student either: even those who discover in the process that they have little aptitude for literary analysis are finding something they are all the better for knowing.

★

Modern practical criticism has evolved from its origins in the 1920s, when I. A. Richards invented it as a rival to literary scholarship. It is no longer a rival, and need not be. It now *uses* literary scholarship. It is an historically informed reading; educationally speaking, a device by which historical knowledge about literary style is imparted.

It is practical in more ways than one, and has many allies. One is textual criticism; and an interest in that can be fostered by reading texts in original spelling and editing them. Another is rhetorical analysis, or an interest in figures of speech such as metaphors, similes and Metaphysical conceits. Another is literary translation; and to examine a poetic version like Dryden's Virgil (1697) or Roy Campbell's Baudelaire (1952) and consider how they might be bettered is to do something more than to advance one's knowledge of Latin or French. It is to train the mind in the uses of literary English too. The technique has now moved far from its point of origin; though without that origin, it could not have moved at all.

As a botanist looks at a garden, an art historian at a painting, or a culinary expert at a meal, so does a practical critic look at a work of literature. And the first mark of the expert is to swallow nothing whole. He looks with an eye to detail. And he knows which details to record, because he knows what questions to ask.

Practical criticism begins with a question, or a series of questions. Art will only look at you if you look at it. But to look is not to stare blankly. Stare at a poem, and it will only stare back. But interrogate it, and it will reply; and progressively reveal itself as it does so.

VERSE

Here are some questions to put to a poem. They are technical questions; but then they can mostly be answered without using a language so technical that few ordinary readers could understand. Terminology may sometimes prove unavoidable, and can be explained as one goes. But it is sensible to insist it should work its passage, and be used only when it has to be used – when familiar terms will not serve at all, or will only serve to a serious loss of brevity.

Such questions are chiefly about formal properties such as metre, vocabulary and syntax. It is the mark of the professional, by and large, to begin with questions of this sort. Amateurs always ask 'What is it about?' or 'Do I like it?' They are both appropriate questions, but there are advantages in deferring them to a later stage in practical criticism. The beginner is right to think such questions matter, but wrong to think they are the place to begin. There is no need to hurry – least of all into hasty and extreme judgements, especially when they are dismissive or damning. The race is less to the swift than to the indefatigable. Judgement will inevitably happen: it cannot and need not be avoided. But it often looks feebly dogmatic to let it all out at once. And it needs to be earned, in the sense that only an analytical groundwork will prove whether the critic is someone who knows enough to make his judgements worth attending to. The expert uses his eyes, unhurriedly. 'Don't think: look', as a philosopher once advised: do not imagine you have the answer before you begin.

An expert, too, knows how not to waste time, and especially the time of those who read him. A poor critique often means an untidily ruminative one; someone has set down the first thing that came to mind about a poem, and then the next, and so on. That represents some sort of thinking; it will do for conversation, though rarely for the best that there is. But then serious conversation is usually an exercise in sincerity. And in criticism sincerity, though a virtue, is not the object of the endeavour. A literary view may be totally sincere and totally wrong.

★

There are certain advantages in starting with metre. For one thing, metre is always a matter of deliberate choice. Nobody, surely, ever wrote a sonnet without consciously intending to write one. Thomas Hardy, who believed one should use all the English metres, wrote metrical outlines, sometimes leaving blanks and sometimes writing nonsense, like an architect sketching out a plan; the details of words could be filled in later. Shelley sometimes knew the metrical shape of his lines before he knew the line itself, as his fragments prove. There is something to be said for beginning with the conscious intention of the poet rather than with more speculative matters. And much to be said for beginning with the obvious. The most important thing about a sonnet, after all, is that it is a sonnet. Form dictates; and to omit all mention of form is to prompt a query in the mind of the reader which is damaging even if unjust: 'Hasn't he noticed?' And to omit all mention till the end might prompt another, and one little less damaging: 'Has he only just noticed?' It is worth daring to be obvious, especially in a first sentence.

The chief forms of English metre or prosody are few, and easily learnt. It is surprising, then, that they are so rarely learnt: in half an hour one can acquire essential equipment for a lifetime.

English verse is accentual, and a foot contains one accented syllable, whether real or notional. Here are the commonest forms.

1. *Blank verse, or five-foot unrhymed lines*: an early Tudor metre that is the chief verse-pattern of Marlowe's plays and Shakespeare's, as well as *Paradise Lost* and many later poems in that tradition, especially extended poems in the eighteenth and nineteenth centuries. The second paragraph of Eliot's *The Waste Land* is a notable twentieth-century

example:

> What are the roots that clutch, what branches grow
> Out of this stony rubbish? Son of man,
> You cannot say, or guess, for you know only
> A heap of broken images . . .

2. *Heroic couplets, or five-foot lines rhyming in pairs*, and called 'heroic' because much seventeenth-century opinion thought them appropriate to the epic, or heroic poem. The metre was first used at length by Chaucer, as the chief form for the *Canterbury Tales*, and dominates much of English verse from Dryden to Crabbe. When Roy Campbell revived it in *The Georgiad* (1931), an attack on London literary life, he was measuring himself ambitiously against the *Dunciad* of Pope:

> Since Georgians are my theme, why should I choose
> Any but the most broadly smiling muse?
> Inspire me, Fun, and set my fancy gliding,
> I'll be your Graves and you my Laura Riding.

3. *Stanzaic forms.* A poem is stanzaic if its metrical pattern is repeated over more than a couplet, the stanzas being visibly separated on the page. A stanzaic poem, for this reason, looks like one even before one has read it: it sits on the page in that way, both in the length of its lines and in its rhyme-pattern.

The commonest stanza is the quatrain, as in Gray's 'Elegy Written in a Country Churchyard', with alternating rhyme:

> The curfew tolls the knell of parting day,
> The lowing herd winds slowly o'er the lea,
> The ploughman homeward plods his weary way,
> And leaves the world to darkness and to me.

Tennyson was to use quatrains with an enclosing rhyme in *In Memoriam*. Another common form is ballad metre, revived in Coleridge's 'Ancient Mariner'.

The commonest stanzas in English, apart from these, are of seven, eight and nine lines. The seven-liner is rhyme royal, as in Chaucer's *Troilus and Criseyde*; the eight is *ottava rima*, borrowed from the Italian epics, as in Byron's *Don Juan*; the nine is the Spenserian, invented for

The Faerie Queene with a long last line of six feet, and often imitated since – notably by Byron in *Childe Harold*. Two eight-liners are buried in Milton's 'Lycidas', and no one knows for certain why they are there.

If an English stanzaic poem does not conform to one of those common types, then there is a fair probability it is unique: something invented by the poet for that poem, and perhaps never imitated since. The great mine of original stanzaic forms in English is Herbert's *Temple*, which consists of 158 poems, 127 of them stanzaic, 98 of them being metrically unique in English. Any modern poet who wanted to adopt or adapt a stanza form should first turn there.

Some prefer to learn the rhyme schemes of these stanzas as letter schemes: rhyme royal, for example, which is so called because James I, King of Scotland, wrote his *Kingis Quair* in that form early in the fifteenth century, imitating Chaucer, rhymes A B A B B C C. All three of the great stanzaic forms end in a couplet. But a much better idea is to learn an example of each form. An instance is of poetic interest in itself, in a way a formula is not; and it stays in the mind longer.

A sonnet or fourteen-liner is not a stanzaic form, though it has often been linked into sequences, like Shakespeare's. It was introduced from Italian poetry by Wyatt, probably in the 1530s, and became an Elizabethan fashion with Sidney's *Astrophel and Stella* (1591). The two chief forms are the Petrarchan and the Shakespearean, and these can be distinguished by the first four lines: the Petrarchan rhymes A B B A, the Shakespearean A B A B. The first eight lines are called the octet; the last six, which show a wide variety of rhyme schemes, the sestet.

Assonance, which is rare in English as a radical device before the present century, is a weak form of rhyme where the accented vowels match, but not the consonants. The safety-belt slogan 'Clunk, click, with every trip', is an instance; it could easily have been made to rhyme, as with 'Clunk, clip . . .', so it must be assumed to be deliberate. Dylan Thomas's 'Fern Hill' is a unique stanzaic poem almost entirely in assonance, though there are rhymes in it for the alert to spot.

★

Metrical analysis is unfashionable because the knowledge it gives is often felt to be inert, in the sense of moving the literary argument nowhere, or nowhere that matters. That is a mistake. It moves argument in two directions, both of them highly rewarding.

First, the metre of a poem, especially if it belongs to a standard type, or varies such a type, sets that poem in a tradition and enables it to be related to that tradition. It is difficult, for example, to write blank verse without exciting comparison with either Shakespeare or Milton, who dominate that metre. A first question, then, to ask of any poem in blank verse and of the last two hundred years is 'Is it more like Shakespeare or Milton, and in which ways?' That would be a good question to put to the second paragraph of Eliot's *The Waste Land*. But one can only ask it at all after noticing that the young Eliot, for all his declared interest in *vers libre*, is indeed writing blank verse. And if the answer is that Eliot is writing Miltonic blank verse rather than Shakespearean, that in its turn gives rise to an interesting chain of argument. In the 1930s Eliot in his criticism was to become an eminent depreciator of Milton. Was he denying a poetic influence he had come to feel had acted too powerfully on his own early poems? And if so, do his later poems, and notably *Four Quartets* (1943), suggest in their metre that he had successfully escaped that influence, or even that he was trying to do so? Practical criticism is no longer the enemy or rival of literary history, as it was in the 1920s. It is now its active ally and guide, as this instance shows. When it analyses the formal properties of literature, it links those properties to their known historical tradition. Every metrical form has a history. Even a unique metrical form, such as a newly invented stanza, stands in some sort of relation to older and more familiar forms.

Second: however unproductive much metrical information may look in itself, it can prove highly rewarding when related to syntax. Syntax is the grammatical shape of a sentence; and sentences sit within the framework of metre in a fascinating variety of ways.

The simplest and most notable instance of the metre–syntax relationship is *enjambement*, or carrying over the sentence without pause from one line to the next. Dryden, in his essay *Of Dramatic Poesy*, calls it 'running the sense into another line'; no term, oddly enough, has ever lastingly replaced the French word in English. The opposite is end-stopped, when the line ends as a syntactical unit. *Enjambement* represents the most striking formal difference between Shakespeare's blank verse and Milton's; and in the century and less between Marlowe and the early Shakespeare in the 1590s and the appearance of *Paradise Lost* in 1667 the formal history of blank verse is largely a history of an expanding tolerance for *enjambement*. Shakespeare inherited from Marlowe a tradition of dramatic verse that is essentially end-stopped:

Was this the face that launched a thousand ships,
And burned the topless towers of Ilium?
Sweet Helen, make me immortal with a kiss.   (v i 98ff.)

Read on in the same speech from Marlowe's *Dr Faustus*, and it offers remarkable instances of *enjambement*, to be recognised less by the mere absence of punctuation than by the magnetic drawing power of the syntax across the lines:

I will be Paris, and for love of thee
Instead of Troy shall Wittenberg be sacked . . .

and again,

Oh, thou art fairer than the evening's air
Clad in the beauty of a thousand stars . . .

That tolerance, then, existed in the English theatre as early as *c* 1590. The decade that followed Marlowe's early death in 1593 was to widen it further. Early Shakespeare employs it only a little more than Marlowe; mid-Shakespeare enlarges it, in the years around the turn of the century; and late Shakespeare allows it abundantly. For an example of early, end-stopped Shakespeare, John of Gaunt's dying speech in *Richard II* will do, at least in its opening lines:

Methinks I am a prophet new inspir'd,
And thus expiring do foretell of him:
His rash fierce blaze of riot cannot last.
For violent fires soon burn out themselves;   (ii i 31–4)

This is a radically different syntactical movement from Cleopatra's elegy on her dead lover in *Antony and Cleopatra*, a play probably written a dozen years later in 1606–7:

His legs bestrid the ocean, his rear'd arm
Crested the world: his voice was propertied
As all the tuned spheres . . .

                              . . . in his livery
        Walk'd crowns and crownets: realms and islands were
        As plates dropp'd from his pocket.   (v ii 82–92)

The first instance there is from subject to verb – '. . . his rear'd arm/
Crested the world' – and among the most daring in English. Half a
century later Milton, who in his sonnets had already followed the Italian fashion of running over from the eighth line to the ninth, a licence
Shakespeare never practised, was to extend the device into a principal
artistic effect. In *Paradise Lost* the plunge of sense across the line-limits
is fully and continuously indulged. In the first six lines of the epic, all
six run over, and all await the long-suspended imperative 'Sing'. The
technical poise is bold and breathtaking, and to begin a work with 'of'
is in itself provocative:

            Of man's first disobedience, and the fruit
            Of that forbidden tree, whose mortal taste
            Brought death into the world, and all our woe
            With loss of Eden, till one greater man
            Restore us, and regain the blissful seat,
            Sing, heavenly muse . . .

But Milton abolished one Shakespearean licence even as he pushed
enjambement to its limits. He forbade himself the feminine ending. A
line is masculine when it ends with an accented syllable, feminine
when it does not. There are few, if any, feminine endings in *Paradise
Lost*: nothing, certainly, like Hamlet's

        To be or not to be: that is the question.
        Whether 'tis nobler in the mind to suffer
        The slings and arrows of outrageous fortune   (iii i 55–7)

The Miltonic reform of Shakespearean metre, then, which dominates
much of eighteenth- and nineteenth-century verse, and especially
blank verse, amounts at its most technical to an extension of *enjambement* and an insistence on masculinity. Cowper's *Task* and
Wordsworth's *Prelude*, not to mention parts of *The Waste Land*, are
metrical outgrowths of *Paradise Lost*. Even the sonnets of Wordsworth
follow Milton rather than Shakespeare, metrically speaking: his
reform survived for much more than a century.

A practical critic of any experience, faced with English verse in these traditional forms, will do something more than read it. He will cast a quick eye down the right-hand side of the page to observe the incidence of *enjambement* and femininity. There are more things to do with poems than to read them through; though reading them through is still the best thing to do with them.

The relation of metre to syntax can be considered in forms other than blank verse. What are the characteristic syntactical units of Dryden's heroic couplets, or of Pope's, and how do they differ? How does this relationship work in Anglo-American verse of the present age, and does it sometimes drive *enjambement* to a point that threatens the integrity of the line? How are subordinate clauses and phrases placed, metrically speaking, in a given poem? These are all questions that require a knowledge of syntax as well as of metre. And syntax is a matter for literary prose as well as for verse; because prose lacks metre, it is often the chief technical issue to arise there. It may be convenient, then, to consider syntax at greater length under another heading.

PROSE

English literary prose of the last four centuries is on the whole harder to discuss or to 'date' than English verse. That is only partly because metre, which is highly informative in an historical sense, is absent from it. It is also because the study of literary syntax lacks all but a handful of terms that are widely accepted and understood. I shall begin with the simplest, illustrating these, where possible, with the openings of classic English novels.

A simple sentence is one without subordinate clauses:

> There was no possibility of taking a walk that day. (Charlotte Brontë, *Jane Eyre*, 1847)

A compound sentence is of more than one clause, linked by a conjunction such as 'and' or 'but':

> Once upon a time, and a very good time it was, there was a moocow coming down along the road, and this moocow that was down along the road met a nicens little boy named baby tuckoo. (James Joyce, *A Portrait of the Artist as a Young Man*, 1916)

A periodic sentence is one with subordinate clauses, and especially one where the subordination is multiple and elaborate:

> It was a bright May morning some twelve years ago, when a youth of still tender age, for he had certainly not entered his teens by more than two years, was ushered into the waiting-room of a house in the vicinity of St James's Square which, though with the general appearance of a private residence, and that too of no very ambitious character, exhibited at this period symptoms of being occupied for some public purpose.　(Disraeli, *Coningsby*, 1844)

An extreme of periodicity, which can hardly be represented by the novel, is 'Ciceronian' English, a prose based on the model of Cicero's most elaborate style where phrases and clauses are built one within another like Chinese boxes: a style apter to an inflected language like Latin than to an uninflected language like English. Hooker is the master of Ciceronian English, and the first sentence of his *Laws of Ecclesiastical Polity* (1593) illustrates this highly suspended syntax:

> Though for no other cause, yet for this, that posterity may know we have not loosely through silence permitted things to pass away as in a dream, there shall be for men's information extant thus much concerning the present state of the Church of God established amongst us, and their careful endeavour which would have upheld the same.

The opening of *Paradise Lost* is a sort of metrical parody of this syntax, which as an expository prose style was dead by the Restoration of 1660. Its opposite is traditionally known as 'Senecan', which is brief and given to simple sentences, like much of Bacon's essays. Some of the elaborations of early seventeenth-century prose, as in Jeremy Taylor or Sir Thomas Browne, have been dubbed baroque on the analogy of the visual arts, and include playfully illusionist effects of syntax.

The Great Divide of English literary prose is the Restoration of 1660, with Dryden as the first master of the new style. The first sentence of the essay *Of Dramatic Poesy* strikes the note: it is in an analytical and explanatory prose that has since, with manifold variations, become the first diplomatic, commercial and scientific language of the world, and it is not a prose that Shakespeare or Milton knew:

It was that memorable day, in the first summer of the late war, when our navy engaged the Dutch: a day wherein the two most mighty and best appointed fleets which any age had ever seen disputed the command of the greater half of the globe, the commerce of nations, and the riches of the universe.

That is a periodic sentence, in its way. But it is not remotely Ciceronian, and there is nothing illusionist about it. Its harmonies are clear almost to the point of austerity; and its functional power, which is what principally impresses, lies in its magisterial ordering. It expounds and explains, and it is a fundamental requirement of any explanation that it should supply the required facts and considerations in the right order. Considered in this practical light, the rich prose of Hooker's *Laws* or of Milton's *Areopagitica* fails. Dryden, Halifax, Addison and Johnson created and refined over a century and more a prose that is masterfully expository. If it is not the world's greatest prose, artistically considered, it is surely its most useful. It is fundamentally 'paratactic', or given to afterthoughts and additions; not 'hypotactic' like Hooker, who inserts detail within detail ('. . . we have not loosely through silence permitted . . . ') to build effects that are massive and yet not readily clear, though always susceptible to learned analysis. The units of the new prose are most characteristically shorter than his. And when they are long, the syntax is never suspended, so that the direction of the sense is always unteasing and largely predictable.

Since the whole of the classic English novel is post-Restoration, the new prose is also the language of English fiction. It is hard to imagine how fiction could have happened at all without the clarification of Restoration syntax. A novel in the style of Bacon is only barely imaginable; in that of Hooker or Milton, hardly imaginable at all. Narration is itself a kind of exposition. It demands an ordering whereby details are placed in a sequence not dominated by an elaborate syntax but required by what the reader needs to understand of an evolving story.

★

Practical criticism is in essence an invitation to look, and look closely, at the language in which poems and prose are written. Its relations with linguistics have already been considered. But one educational relation is in any case clear. To be interested in a language, whether one's native language or another, is to be interested in how thoughts can be expressed in it. 'How would you say that in French?' would be the obsessive question of anyone seriously learning French; if he wanted to learn it fast, he would ask that question of his own stream of consciousness, translating his own thoughts into another language in his idler moments as well as in those formally dedicated to translation.

The language of a given author, to a lesser extent, is like another language, and the linguistic obsession can profitably work here as well. 'How would Shakespeare (or Milton) say that?' and 'What did he mean when he wrote . . . ?' Vocabulary, or the study of individual words, is one aspect of such questions; metre is another. But at its most advanced and rewarding, practical criticism is a matter of whole sentences and groups of sentences. That is why the short poem is its most natural unit of study. To bring the arts of grammatical analysis to bear upon literary language, where 'grammar' is understood as widely as that, is the task in view.

7 How to Work: or Using a Library

How index learning turns no student pale,
Yet holds the eel of science by the tail.

Pope, The Dunciad, I 279–80

Half a word, fixed on or near the spot, is worth a cart-load of
recollection.

Thomas Gray, letter of 6 September 1758

Many a man can travel to the very bourne of heaven, and yet
want confidence to put down his half-seeing.

John Keats, letter of 3 February 1818

If one is a critic or an historian of literature, to have an idea is to want
to be in a library. The sensation, as Henry James once remarked, is 'as
interesting as an unopened telegram'. An idea means a question one
eagerly wants an answer to, or a hunch one burns to verify. If the critic
is without an idea, on the other hand, then a library is just the place to
get out of.

This chapter supposes the idea to be there, and so insistently there
that it will not go away. And it assumes, however optimistically, that a
good academic library is to hand. The question can be answered, it
seems natural to hope, or the hunch confirmed, by tracking the answer down from article to article or from book to book. That is often a
reasonable hope, as things are. Literary studies now possess an abun-
dance of reference aids, none better than those that serve English.
Indeed it is now clear that English in the present century has
equipped itself with historical dictionaries and bibliographies
superior to those of any other living language – though it cannot realistically hope to rival the completeness of reference that distinguishes

those most dignified of dead literary languages, Latin or classical Greek.

The first rule of a scholarly existence is that the sun should not go down on an unanswered question, unless it absolutely must. You learn a language best by looking up the words and phrases you do not know. You learn a literature by a similar sort of assiduous curiosity. That is why a literary scholar in the making trains himself by keeping whatever works of reference he can afford to possess near at hand, and by using them the moment a question arises. The *Oxford Dictionary of English Etymology* (1966) by C. T. Onions and others is an even better one-volume lexicon for a man of letters than the more familiar *Concise Oxford English Dictionary* (1911, etc.) or the *Shorter OED* (2 vols, 1933, etc.). That is because etymologies are both fascinating in themselves and one of the best ways of retaining a word in the mind. Other great works of reference have been similarly epitomised for the ordinary reader. Even the vast *Dictionary of National Biography* (1885–1909), to which a number of supplements have been added since 1909, most recently by decades, has been abbreviated as the *Concise DNB*; and the *Cambridge Bibliography of English Literature* (4 vols, 1940), which has since been revised as *New CBEL 600–1950* (5 vols, 1969–77), exists in miniature as *Concise CBEL 600–1950* (1958, revised 1965). In no other modern literature is it as easy as in English to discover the essential facts about either words or works.

The second rule of life, and one to be acquired more slowly, is to learn how to move briskly from one work to another. An experienced scholar uses books orchestrally, so to speak, or in wide combinations. He needs runs of works, not just individual books. He ranges, as he works, the length and breadth of a library, passing rapidly from reference to article to book to article to reference, and settling only briefly on any one of them. The spectacle can be at once inspiriting and disturbing to a beginner, who often imagines that scholars of great eminence study works from start to finish. The truth is that they do not – not, at least, if they can find a way to escape it. In his own leisure, a professional scholar may read enormously, perusing in the ordinary way from the beginning of a book to the end. But in a library, at least, he rarely settles for long or reads at length. That is why literary scholarship is so much less of a sedentary occupation than outsiders suppose, and why it calls for physical fitness as well as mental agility. A literary scholar needs stamina. Watch him at work in a great collection such as the Reading Room of the British Library in Bloomsbury, and see how often he is on his feet to consult a book on the open shelves or to ask a question of a staff-member or fellow-reader. He is probably not wasting time even when he is in the coffee room, if he is talking shop there; and literary scholars do mostly talk shop. Even at his desk, his eyes move alertly from the page he is writing to the several books he has to hand.

The beginner, by contrast, often finds himself frustrated when he tries to sit in a reading-room and read something through in the order in which it is printed. A library, for all but the most concentrated minds, is usually too distracting a place for that. Only a beginner, in any case, would have failed to notice that most books have tables of contents, and that many have indexes. They are there to save him time that he can use to consult other tables and other indexes. If a book must be read all the way through, as narratives such as plays and novels must, then a library is not usually the best place to read it in.

DICTIONARIES

A dictionary is not just a place to discover what a word means, or how to pronounce it. It can also be used as an inexhaustible aid which is at once historical and critical. In every generation in this century there has been a handful of scholars to notice that the great *Oxford English Dictionary* is a rich mine of critical evidence still largely unworked by historians of literature. A few even notice that the prefaces to its early volumes, present in the first edition that began to appear in 1888 but dropped from the corrected reissue of 1933, contain unique information about the history of the language. But then it is a rare scholar indeed that so much as glances at the preface to any work of reference, even if it is to a work he happens to own. Most of us, as we work with words, miss most of the available chances. And yet any reference book, rightly considered, is a device for making one appear more learned than one is, for acknowledging that debt, and for becoming more learned in the very act of appearing to be so. And no work can do all that better than this dictionary.

The first information offered by an historical dictionary such as this, after the pronunciation of a word, is its derivation. Since etymology (from Greek *etumos* = real, true; and *logos* = word) is absorbing in itself, and the theme of at least one radio game, 'My Word', with a vast national audience, it is odd that any student of literature should need persuading that it is interesting. But there are two powerful reasons for concerning oneself with etymology, apart from the joy of the thing itself. One is that etymology is highly mnemonic – so much so that it is often hard to retain a word that one has newly learned, such as one from Chaucer or the *Gawain* poet, unless one attends to its origins at the same time. The other is that it demonstrates how much and how often English words have altered their meanings down the ages: not only from Old English to Middle English to modern, but within modern English itself. That truth must remain obscure, and even unnoticed, unless words are studied for what they are: little histories in themselves. C. S. Lewis's *Studies in Words* (1960, enlarged 1967) is an exciting model here: it offers little histories of 'nature', 'wit', 'sense', 'life' and other key terms, working lexicography and intellectual development into a single pattern of argument.

The rewards can be small or great. When Polonius exclaims triumphantly, in *Hamlet*: 'Still harping on my daughter' (ii ii 189), a twentieth-century audience will understand 'still' in its present sense, which happens by an unlucky chance to fit Shakespeare's context here. In fact it more probably means 'always' or 'continually', as it commonly does in Renaissance English. Andrew Marvell, in 'Upon Appleton House', describes Lord Fairfax's country house in these terms:

> A stately frontispiece of poor
> Adorns without the open door,

meaning that the poor await the alms of a generous patron. The first two senses of 'frontispiece' in the *OED* are both architectural, meaning façade or pediment. The sense of the first page of a book, which is now the most familiar, is admittedly recorded by the dictionary as earlier than Marvell's poem, in 1614; but it probably needs to be resisted here, tempting as it is to see the remark as a bookish metaphor – the more so since the poem continues in a vein that relates people to things:

> Nor less the rooms within commends
> Daily new furniture of friends.

King Lear ends with an exchange of remarks between bystanders, viewing the old king with the dead Cordelia in his arms, that can easily be heard or read in a manner that misses the point:

Kent   Is this the promis'd end?
Edgar   Or image of that horror? (v iii 265–6)

'Image' does not mean a figure of speech in Renaissance English; its
sense is still close to Latin *imago*, and it means a portrait or likeness,
usually a painting or statue. So Edgar is pointing to a tableau of father
and daughter, probably set centre-stage, that reminds him of the end
of the world promised in Scripture. And sometimes meanings can
overlap and coexist, old and new together: 'horrid', for example, in
Shakespeare and Milton, often means what it means today, or meant
before it was weakened into colloquial cant: fearful. But Latin *horridus*
meant bristling, shaggy or standing on end; and this is how Spenser
uses it in *The Faerie Queene*:

>His haughty helmet, horrid all with gold,
>Both glorious brightness, and great terror bred   (i vii 31),

where the two senses of 'bristling' and 'fearful' are ingeniously linked.
Dryden and Pope later use the word in a knowingly archaic way:

>Horrid with fern, and intricate with thorn,

and

>Ye grots and caverns shagg'd with horrid thorn!

Samuel Johnson's poem of 1783, 'On the Death of Dr Robert Levet',
is in a memorably lapidary style. But it is more memorable still if one
recognises that some of its terms stand closer to their Latin origins
there than they now do:

>Well tried through many a varying year,
>   See Levet to the grave descend;
>Officious, innocent, sincere,
>   Of ev'ry friendless name the friend.

Officium means duty, and *nocere* is the verb to harm. Even the third epi-
thet gains from a sense of its etymology, which is based on a Latin
adjective meaning 'clean, pure, whole'. To read that line with a sense
of history is to realise the inadequacy of structuralism: how little an

advanced literary language represents a single or arbitrary system that stands in relation to nothing but itself.

The best game of all, and the most useful in its results, is to show the *OED* to be mistaken or inadequate in detail. The game is abundantly played, often as philological parody, in J. R. R. Tolkien's *The Lord of the Rings* (1954–5), where words, meanings and origins not sanctioned in the dictionary are solemnly or playfully proposed. A serious discovery in this field might be communicated to the editors at the Clarendon Press, Oxford, who are already at work on a supplement that began to appear in 1972 and will have to be kept in repair. The periodical *Notes and Queries*, edited from Pembroke College, Oxford, appears every two months, often recording senses earlier than those recorded in the dictionary, and it tries to answer readers' queries and to announce new discoveries. 'Hobbit', a word that gave its name to Tolkien's first story (1937), was until recently without a known origin, and the author himself is said to have forgotten where he found it, until an *OED* correspondent reported he had found it in a work of Victorian folklore, *The Denham Tracts* (1892–5) (*The Times*, 31 May 1977).

Some of the omissions of the dictionary are more surprising. It includes an article on 'momently' that astonishingly omits the only notable instance of the word in English literature, in Coleridge's 'Kubla Khan':

> And mid these dancing rocks at once and ever
> It flung up momently the sacred river,

though it quotes from Coleridge's Satyrane's Letters as they appeared in his *Biographia Literaria* (1817). But it misinterprets the word as meaning 'enduring only for a moment'; whereas it meant for Coleridge what it meant in the very seventeenth-century instances that the dictionary quotes: intermittent, or from moment to moment. The passage, as it appears in the most recent edition of Coleridge's letters, was written to his wife from Germany in September 1798, several months after the probable date of 'Kubla Khan', and soon after crossing the North Sea:

> The ocean is a noble thing by night: a beautiful white cloud of foam, at momently intervals, roars and rushes by the side of the vessel, and stars of flame dance and sparkle and go out in it – and every

now and then light detachments of foam dart away from the vessel's
side with their galaxies of stars, and scour out of sight, like a Tartar
troop over a wilderness . . .   (*Collected Letters* [1956–71] I 416)

The Khan was a Tartar emperor, so it looks as if a sea-journey had
triggered more than one recollection of the poem in his fertile mind.

BIBLIOGRAPHIES

Apart from the *New Cambridge Bibliography of English Literature*
(1969–77), which is concerned with British and Irish authors established by 1950, English is now increasingly well equipped with individual author-bibliographies, such as the Soho Bibliographies of
Edmund Burke, Henry James, Ezra Pound and D. H. Lawrence.
Such bibliographies are listed author by author in the *New CBEL*,
where they exist, and in the *Concise CBEL*, which deals with about four
hundred authors in one volume.

An author-bibliography can offer information of far wider interest
than the physical attributes of books or their locations, i.e. details concerning where copies are to be found. They can sometimes be the best
literary study that there is. As an example, Richard L. Purdy's
Thomas Hardy: A Bibliographical Study (1954, corrected 1968) is a mine
of knowledge about Hardy's literary revisions, and especially about
the differences between a version of a novel as it appeared serially, or
in a periodical, and as it eventually appeared as a book. Such works
are well provided with an apparatus to explain their own procedures,
so that a familiarity with the physical aspects of books can be acquired
by using them gently, progressively and intelligently. The best way to
learn about such matters is to study them in the case of an author one
already respects. As an auxiliary, the most attractive of all introductions to this subject remains John Carter's *ABC for Book-Collectors*
(1952, etc.), a handbook wittily laid out as an instance of the very fea-
tures it describes. There is no need to be a book-collector in order to
enjoy it.

'Bibliography' is by now an irreversibly ambiguous word, and
especially in British usage. It can mean either the study of books as
physical objects, as in Carter's *ABC*, or a list like the *New CBEL*.
Americans, to avoid that ambiguity, would call the *New CBEL* a
checklist. My concern here is with the second sense of the word, or
with literary lists, whether chronological or alphabetical. Some of the
best of these are not called bibliographies at all.

Only one great national library in Britain, now known as the British Library, publishes its catalogue. The *General Catalogue* of the British Museum is now largely complete in a massive edition that began in 1965 and is subject to recurring supplements; and it often contains the most complete list available in print of certain English and even foreign authors. Many academic libraries now possess it, if only to assist their administrative processes, and especially so since the appearance of a convenient compact edition. An even vaster work, the *National Union Catalog* (1968–), aims to list all reported holdings in United States and Canadian libraries, based on Library of Congress cards, and though it makes no claims to completeness it can often be a good place to start.

What is more, English is now the best organised vernacular literature for finding-lists of books that function by period, and especially for the first two centuries of printing. The newly revised *Short-title Catalogue of Books Printed in England, Scotland and Ireland 1475–1640* (2 vols, 1976–) lists all books published in the British Isles, regardless of language, between Caxton and Charles I's recall of Parliament; and its sequel by Donald Wing on 1641–1700 has already begun to appear in revision (1972–). In principle, at least, it is now possible to find a copy of every English book published before 1700, whether in a British or American library, and the abbreviations 'STC' and 'Wing', followed by a number, are internationally accepted as referring to these standard works of reference.

CONCORDANCES AND INDEXES

A concordance is an alphabetical list of every word in an author or book, or at least of every significant word. It is usually confined to a single author, most commonly a poet; though there are now a few prose concordances, such as one for Malory and another for James Joyce's *Finnegans Wake*, and a few that treat more than one author together, like Herbert S. Donow's *A Concordance to the Sonnet Sequences of Daniel, Drayton, Shakespeare, Sidney and Spenser* (1969).

An index is an alphabetical list of names and, less often and less reliably, of topics. They are commonest in discursive works, and rarest in novels, though a few indexed novels exist: Samuel Richardson, for example, equipped *Clarissa* with an appendix of 'moral and instructive sentiments', indexed, and *Sir Charles Grandison* with an 'Index Historical and Characteristical' that included abstractions as well as names.

Everyone active in literary studies knows, in a general way, that these aids exist. They are a familiar fact of life. But somehow their use is still underrated. I propose here to look at some of their odder virtues and less familiar uses.

A concordance can help to show what a word means by establishing what it regularly or usually means elsewhere in works by the same author, or by contemporary authors. Consider again Polonius's use of 'still', in *Hamlet*: if all the other instances suggest the sense of 'always' in Shakespeare, then the case for supposing it means that in Polonius's mouth is so much the stronger, though still not utterly conclusive. It would be stronger still if backed by evidence from contemporary poets, of a sort that the *OED* or Donow's concordance provides.

Again, a concordance is a ready guide to word frequency. This is a delicate issue, and needs to be governed by a sense of reasonable probability. Frequency tables now exist for some of these purposes. English studies are still far from achieving a reliable statistical study of vocabulary; if they are to move convincingly in that direction, then they will need even more concordances than we are so far provided with, and frequency tables that clearly establish the average probabilities for the use of a word within its genre and period.

An index, too, can be a major literary aid. Perhaps the two greatest indexes in English studies in the present age have been Esmond de Beer's index to Evelyn's diary (1955) and L. F. Powell's to Boswell's *Life of Johnson* (1934–50), which includes more than the life itself. The article on 'poetry' in the Boswell index, for example, would be indispensable to any intelligent research into Johnson's view of the matter: 'no necessity for . . . mediocre poetry entitled to esteem . . . cannot be translated . . . what is poetry? . . . cannot be defined . . . devotional poetry unsatisfactory or undesirable . . . compared with lexicography. . . .'

OTHER AIDS

The language of poetry can be investigated through references in other directions. Renaissance poetry, especially, is now recognised as highly allusive in its relations to popular speech, and some of the hidden surfaces of Wyatt, Donne, Shakespeare and Herbert can be brought to light by using Morris P. Tilley's *A Dictionary of the Proverbs in English in the Sixteenth and Seventeenth Centuries* (1950). This is the posthumous work of an American scholar, and was used by

F. P. Wilson in his revision of *The Oxford Dictionary of English Proverbs* (1970), which also appeared posthumously. Wilson's long interest in the subject can best be studied in his 'Proverbial Wisdom of Shakespeare', reprinted in his *Shakespearian and Other Studies* (1969).

The use of emblems throughout Europe has been codified by Arthur Henkel and A. Schöne in their *Emblemata* (1967), an illustrated guide to sixteenth- and seventeenth-century emblems and their literary uses; it has a thematic index in German, among other indexes, but unfortunately no author index.

Novels and novelists have long been subjects for reference aids; indeed the activity is more characteristic of the Victorians than of the present century, and has grown less than other branches of the subject. There are numerous Victorian and Edwardian guides to great nineteenth-century novelists, of which perhaps the best is Gilbert A. Pierce's *The Dickens Dictionary* (1872, etc.) which summarises plots, lists characters alphabetically within novels with generous extracts, and includes 'A Classed List of Characters', so that one can tell at a glance how many parish clerks there are in Dickens's novels, how many murderers, and how many old maids. There are also numerous guides to fiction in general: perhaps the most useful is Ernest A. Baker's *A Guide to Historical Fiction* (1914), arranged country by country; the first section, on the British Isles, lists historical novels by order of the period with which they deal, from Roman Britain down to the Victorian age.

Periodicals, by contrast, have had to wait until recently before receiving similar attention, and even now they remain of all literary sources the hardest and most demanding to explore. For just this reason, however, they are of all printed sources the likeliest to yield original and unnoticed results. The great age of the British literary and political periodical began with the foundation of the *Edinburgh Review* in 1802, but the riches of periodical literature in the nineteenth and twentieth centuries will always prove difficult to bring under control. Two resolute attempts are now in progress. The first is Walter E. Houghton's *Wellesley Index to Victorian Periodicals 1824–1900* (1966–), which contains abundant new identifications of the authorship of articles in an age in which literary reviewing was still mainly anonymous. The second is Marion Sader's *Comprehensive Index to English-language Little Magazines 1890–1970* (1976–), which lists authors, mainly American, alphabetically grouping their own works with reviews and other secondary materials.

Perhaps only two other works of reference need be commended here, both of them general. One is D. C. Browning's revision of John W. Cousin's *Dictionary of Literary Biography, English & American*, first published in its new form by Everyman's Library in 1958; and *Annals of English Literature 1475–1950*, which was largely revised by R. W. Chapman for its second edition of 1961. This is a chronological list of literary events, year by year, with marginal data concerning events from political and social history that coincide, and so arranged that the happenings of any one year can be seen at a glance; it is a less amusing book, if more instantly useful, than *The Book of Days*, edited by Robert Chambers (2 vols, 1863–4), which treats historical events day by day through the calendar, from January to December.

8   *How to Write:*
or the Use of English

I prophesy the unparalleled embarrassment of a battalion of harassed postillions gauging the symmetry of a potato peeled by a lovable but grisly sibyl.

Bertrand Russell's spelling test

When a man has anything of his own to say, and is really in earnest that it should be understood, he does not usually make cavalry regiments of his sentiments, and seek abroad for sesquipedalian words.

Charles Dickens, 'Saxon-English', *Household Words* (1858)

. . . To gradual Time's last gift, a written speech
Wrought of high laughter, loveliness and ease.

W. B. Yeats, 'Upon a House Shaken by the Land Agitation'

This chapter gives practical advice about critical essays, and how to write them.

★

The hardest part of writing is to write: thinking is much easier. Beginners often suppose that it is originality of mind that counts most in the life of an author, and it is lucky for us all that this is not so. If it were, life would be largely empty even for a genius. For though we think all the time, original ideas of consequence are far rarer than lifetimes. Einstein was once asked what one should do with an original idea, and replied after some thought: 'I don't know. I only ever had one.'

A good idea for a critical essay, realistically considered, is something a great deal less than what happened to Einstein once in his lifetime. To a mind sensitively adaptive, it commonly means an idea based on something one has heard or read that can be made to go somewhere: to grow into something more than it already is. It bears an intimate relation to existing knowledge, and that relation needs to be stated; but it also hopes to exceed it, if only by a little. Knowledge moves onwards by inches as well as by leaps, and the most reasonable ambition here is to edge it forward beyond some known point. Plagiarism is something else. It means copying without acknowledgement, and is a kind of theft. But the adaptive instinct that lies at the heart of a good critical essay is more like borrowing and returning with interest.

Writing is hard. It sometimes seems even harder than it is, because one can easily forget it is not a single process. Those who say they cannot write, and give up too soon, usually mean they cannot write good prose in a single process. They badly need to be told that hardly anybody can. Professional writers with years of experience behind them often regard three versions as a bare minimum, and five to seven versions are not uncommon. And just because the hardest thing in writing is to write, it needs more time to be done well, or even decently, than the beginner is inclined to allow. Trying to write can mean discovering, and with a jolt, how much one still has to learn about one's own native language. The art of composition can make one feel a foreigner to one's own tongue: a disturbing experience. Such is the shock of moving from speaking to writing. And it explains why the act of composition itself needs to be taken more seriously than it often is; why it needs to be allowed more time; and why revision is a necessary element, even to the most experienced. All that profits one more than amassing ever more evidence or erecting still more supporting arguments. One needs to stop reading and start writing at a stage early enough to give one's own prose a chance.

When a subject is called English, all that advice is more than ordinarily true. No one is likely to respect the literary views of one who writes bad prose. Incompetent style invites mockery here, and for good reason; and professional bodies are understandably contemptuous of illiteracy and expressive inefficiency in those claiming to be qualified in a modern language, especially if it is their own. Critical style is vulnerable. It is closely scanned for evidence of literary ability, and it needs in a highly special sense to justify itself as it goes.

More than that, the style of criticism affects and qualifies the kind of credence one gives it. Critical style does not need to be good in a copy-book sense; but it emphatically needs to be good in its own way. That way affects the assertions it makes, and controls the response of those who read it. Sir Philip Sidney's aristocratic assurance in the opening to his *Apology for Poetry* ('When the right virtuous Edward Wotton and I were at the Emperor's court together, we gave ourselves to learn horsemanship . . .'), or the witty dogmatism that marks the best of Samuel Johnson, or Coleridge's buttonholing urgency in the *Biographia Literaria*, all govern the reaction of the reader and power-fully influence him to accept or demur.

This account of critical writing will begin with some elementary reflections, and work outwards towards others that are wider and more speculative.

PUNCTUATION

There is something to be said for using all that there is, or nearly all. English is not so abundantly endowed with 'points' that one can easily afford to dispense with any of them. And punctuation helps to compensate for the serious losses of written and printed language as against speech: losses of intonation, timing and pausing that can help to make spoken language animated and telling. Prose is impoverished when it is set up entirely between full stops and commas, and the total effect of that impoverishment is soporific.

Other punctuations than the comma, then, are worth attending to. A colon often precedes an instance, or a precision of something more generally stated, as in the paragraph above; or a quotation; or a list, whether of words, or phrases, or clauses. It may also, in a syntactical pattern now rarely used, divide an antithesis, as in Sydney Smith's epigram: 'Science is his forte: omniscience his foible.' A semi-colon has intermediate power between a stop and a comma, as this sentence illustrates; and it can be neatly added in revision as a final after-thought, by over-stopping a comma that needs to carry more weight than any comma properly can. Evelyn Waugh's aphorism would be less witty with a comma than with a semi-colon: 'We are all born Americans; but we die French.' Dashes can be more expressive than brackets to distinguish a parenthesis; and the single dash, or 'dashing dash', can introduce an afterthought – provided it is not overplayed. A question mark does what it says.

Only three devices of this sort are worth avoiding in formal prose: the exclamation mark, which looks strident and over-obvious in the context of critical persuasion; underlining for emphasis, which amounts to an admission of syntactical failure – though it *can* justify itself in an emergency where an ambiguity desperately needs to be avoided; and the apostrophe, other than for genitives. Whatever Bernard Shaw may have done in his prefaces, formal prose looks better without 'it's' and 'don't' – contractions that force upon the reader a usage he would rather feel free to adopt or ignore for himself.

Titles

There is a large difference between Hamlet and *Hamlet*, and it can be all the difference between sense and nonsense. On the page, however, only a settled convention like underlining can clarify the difference between a character and a play. In this respect, at least, written language is more expressive than spoken.

Book titles should be underlined. Titles of parts of books, such as short poems, are better within single inverted commas. Never use both. The formal distinction between Wordsworth's *Prelude* and his 'Tintern Abbey' is informative. Titles that are essentially descriptive and traditional, like Shakespeare's sonnets or the Book of Genesis, are better left so.

In critical prose, titles are normally 'short', or abbreviated from the title-page in a self-sufficient way. Wordsworth's *Prelude,* when it appeared posthumously in 1850, was entitled *The Prelude, or the Growth of a Poet's Mind: an Autobiographical Poem*, but it would ordinarily be pedantic to call it anything but *The Prelude* or the *Prelude*. Defoe's *Robinson Crusoe* bore in its first edition of 1719 a title of sixty-eight words, but is now commonly described in two.

Titles in English are largely capitalised, those in other languages usually not, for example Proust's *A la recherche du temps perdu*; though there is a growing tendency towards fewer capitals in English too. A colon should precede a subtitle, where a subtitle is needed.

Quotations

These are best kept short. And they should be instantly to the point at issue, and not just vaguely illustrative. The shorter the better, and the more intimately interwoven with argument the better. Though modern educative theory has vastly underrated memory in general, it has paradoxically overrated it here. Any ordinary literary memory is capacious enough to carry, and without exceptional effort, the quotations that a critical essay needs to make it specific. They are often no more than phrase-long, after all. The real case for learning poems by heart, which is an excellent one, is quite unconnected with this: it rather concerns the sort of critical rumination and comparison that only a well-stocked mind can undertake.

Discussions of prose, even of novels, can benefit, too, from the specificity of a remembered quotation. There is no remarkable memory feat involved in recalling Conrad's 'jungle without a policeman', E. M. Forster's 'Only connect', or Jane Austen's opening account of Emma as 'handsome, clever, and rich'; their service in critical argument is to make argument particular – to unwaffle. The intelligent reader of novels effortlessly knows from memory not whole sentences or paragraphs, but words and phrases in significant contexts.

Brief quotations are kept within the text, in single inverted commas, especially if in prose. Verse quotations of more than one line, and prose of length, should be taken out of the text and indented without inverted commas. A colon precedes a quotation, unless it is syntactically merged into the sentence. References to well-known texts like Shakespeare's plays or Milton's *Paradise Lost* should be to the most familiar citation: act, scene and line for plays; book and line for epics, and so on. Quotations from novels can be cited by number of chapter only. Most such references can be tacked immediately after the quotation in brackets, e.g. (ix 327–9), and footnotes should be kept to the minimum.

STYLE

The first aim is to be brief. A short sentence is more telling than a long one, especially at the start of an essay. A two-word sentence, which is about as short as a sentence can be in formal prose, would perhaps startle immoderately. Long sentences, especially when they stand early in an essay, tire and repel the reader, unless arbitrated by a syntax as assured as Gibbon's or Macaulay's. In beginner-prose they more often look indecisive, woolly and blindly flailing. Good critical prose is short and sharp, as in the best traditions of the higher professions: law, medicine, the civil service. A notice once found in post offices illustrates how excellent such prose can be:

Postmasters are neither bound to give change nor authorised to demand it.

That is the perfect expository sentence: brisk, dense, clear and auth-oritative. Not one word in it could be changed or re-ordered for the better. For less demanding models, though still lofty in their excel-lence, try A. E. Housman's *Selected Prose* (1961), which includes criti-cal reviews, addresses and prefaces from 1890 to his death in 1936; or George Orwell's critical essays of the 1930s and 1940s, which have often been anthologised.

Brevity goes by paragraphs as well as sentences, and it matters in both. An argument is the clearer and the cleaner for moving in separ-able stages. The more sharply demarcated those stages, the better; and a paragraph break is one way of demarcating. That is why re-vision often takes the form of shortening sentences and paragraphs. Revision simplifies – and for some extraordinary reason simplicity is the hardest of all stylistic effects to achieve, and the one that takes longest. It has to be worked for, and worked for hard. The effect of careless ease comes last.

The parts of speech differ significantly in value. The noun is plainly the most overrated today, and the most over-worked in fashionable critical prose, and even more so in American prose than in British. Abstract nouns are the most over-worked of all. Linguists call this vice of style 'nominality', a word which is itself an instance of what it de-scribes: it is long, learned and abstract. Some prose could benefit by conferring a greater role on the adjective, remembering that in English, as in many other languages, any adjective can function as a noun, as in Shakespeare's *Tempest*:

In the dark *backward* and abysm of time   (i ii 50)

The verb, too, is weakly underplayed in much modern prose. Con-sider these two workaday instances of administrative language:

This report is an abridgement of an earlier report . . .

and

This report *abridges* another . . .,

where the second is plainly a stronger formulation, throwing more weight on the verb, and a transitive verb at that: 'is an abridgement of' amounts to nominality run to seed. And nouns are the more telling for not being abstract, by and large: 'It was like a dream' is stronger than 'It had a dream-like quality.' Only personal nouns, what is more, properly take the genitive 's', outside headlines: 'the poet's meaning' is acceptable English; but 'the meaning of the poem' requires an 'of'.

It would be instructive to compile a list of stylistic elements that make for the vacuous and the soporific in expository prose, especially when they are amassed together: nouns, and above all abstractions; verbs in the passive mood; and long sentences and long paragraphs. Contrast the sort of prose that is welcoming to the reader and enlivening to pursue: aptly energetic in its verbs, unabstracted, active in mood, and brief both by sentences and by paragraphs. The opening of George Orwell's essay on Dickens (1939) illustrates the pace and verve that good critical prose can have:

Dickens is one of those writers who are well worth stealing. Even the burial of his body in Westminster Abbey was a species of theft, if you come to think of it.

That is the entire first paragraph. Now consider Simon Gray's parody of student prose in his play *Butley* (1971):

Hermione's re-awakening – the statue restored to life after a winter of sixteen years' duration – is in reality Leontes's re-awakening, spiritually, and of course the most moving exemplification of both the revitalization theme and thus of forgiveness in the theological as well as the human level. The central image is drawn from nature, to counterpoint the imagery of the first half of the play, with its stress on sickness and deformity . . . (Act II)

Of these seventy words of near-nonsense on *The Winter's Tale*, seventeen are abstractions, or about a quarter. Some are totally meaningless, like 'duration', and could be simply struck out; others are misused, like 'reality' and 'nature'. 'Of course' and 'thus' are clear evidences of fumbling, and they are well worth avoiding altogether. The dramatic parody is just, though cruel. Nobody who read this essay could feel sure the author knew what 'spiritually' or 'counterpoint' mean. It is doubtful if anything is said at all.

Vocabulary

This is an aspect of style, but it may be convenient to segregate it. Like most advice about words, it is mainly negative.

It might be good to start a fashion, in vocabulary or elsewhere; but it looks merely weak-minded to follow one. There are always fashionable words worth avoiding, and words that were recently fashionable are even better worth avoiding. What is needed here is a grey list, not a black one: a good writer can after all make something of a bad word. But he needs to be conscious of the task, and of how difficult it is.

In critical prose these words are promising candidates for any grey list:

> valid *and* validity
> > relevant *and* relevance
> > > viable
> > > > meaningful
> > > > > societal (*for* social)
> > > > > > parameter
> > > > > > > structure (*especially as a verb*)
> > > > > > > > overall (*for* total *or* general)
> > > > > > > > > ongoing (*for* continuous *or* continuing)

and one might add 'thus', especially at the beginning of sentences. 'I' and 'we', though sometimes difficult to avoid, are better used sparingly.

Design

Ancient and Renaissance critics often divided authorship into three stages: invention, disposition and style. Beginners often forget the second, and imagine that writing means having something to say and saying it well, in a sentence-by-sentence sense. But the worst problems of authorship lie rather in disposition, or design, or arrangement. Most people have something worth saying, and many can write sentences. The grand difficulty of authorship, as any working author knows, is getting things in the right order. If that difficulty is not faced early, it is all too easy to retire defeated, imagining oneself to be stupider than one is.

The best way to order things is in one's head: to work them out at what look like idle moments, like waiting for a bus – first this point, then that, and concluding with . . . . That is what many a public speaker and many a journalist does, arranging in his mind what Dryden used to call 'the heads of the argument'. The second best way is the 'back-of-an envelope', where any piece of paper can be used to arrange a case for those whose thoughts are not yet so advanced, or whose memories are so weak, that they cannot depend on mental power alone. The third way, which can be essential where a body of documentation is involved, is to assemble materials in an argumentative order as one reads; but in that case it is important to take notes not in the form one thinks of them or finds them, but rather in the order in which they are likely to be needed as one writes. In critical reading, one rarely comes upon the points one will use in just the order they will be used in.

A traditional way of organising one's own thoughts, and other people's, is by keeping a commonplace book. Renaissance men of letters often kept them; so do some modern poets, as W. H. Auden's published commonplace book *A Certain World* (1971) shows. A commonplace book collects significant passages one has read, and one's own reflections, under general headings. Quotations need to be referenced, in that case: one will need the reference in quoting, and it serves to remind that the thoughts of others are not one's own. Much of Coleridge's innocent plagiarism arose from his failure to observe that rule. But Shakespeare's advice in his 77th sonnet is still good:

> Look what thy memory cannot contain
> Commit to these waste blanks, and thou shalt find
> Those children nurs'd, deliver'd from thy brain,
> To take a new acquaintance of thy mind.
>   These offices, so oft as thou wilt look,
>   Shall profit thee, and much enrich thy book.

The design of a critical essay is exceptional. For one thing, it is not entirely usual in authorship, apart from journalism, to put one's conclusion in the opening sentence – though Homer's *Iliad* and Shakespeare's *Romeo and Juliet* begin in this way. A critical essay best begins like *Romeo and Juliet*:

> . . . A pair of star-cross'd lovers take their life . . .   (Prologue 6)

Suspense, whether narrative or argumentative, is none the less that because the reader is presented with the conclusion at the start. An efficiently organised essay needs to present its reason for existing in its first sentence, or at the very latest in its first paragraph. The reader needs to be given a reason for reading on: and in the case of criticism, the reason is that a certain conclusion is about to be demonstrated. 'Prove *that* . . .', the reader may murmur sceptically to himself. If the conclusion is hard to prove, or far from self-evident, so much the better. For all these reasons, introductions that generalise widely or merely warm up the pen of the writer are best avoided; and if drafted at all, it is often a good idea to delete them in revision.

Secondary materials, or the writings of other critics, can shape an argument to real advantage. If an essay is an argument at all, then it is against something: preferably against a view widely or at least influentially held. And that view, defective or incomplete as it is, needs to be stated at an early stage, and specifically, so that the reader can see who the adversary is. There is no advantage in shadow-boxing: if T. S. Eliot was wrong about *Hamlet*, then Eliot's name, and the title and source of his essay, and its date, all need to be mentioned. Criticism is not good to the extent that it is true, or worthless to the extent that it is false, though issues of truth and falsehood clearly arise. It can help prodigiously by being mistaken: honestly or dishonestly mistaken, mistaken in all innocence or through palpable prejudice. And to write a critical essay that is truly one's own needs the sense of direction that the criticism of another can give, just as a good conversationalist needs to be a good listener too. Criticism is a conversation, a to-and-fro, though as critics we converse with the dead such as Aristotle and Johnson as well as with the living. It cannot flourish in an introspective or purely ruminative frame of mind. It is polemical, not a species of soliloquising. And one can no more do it alone than one can play tennis alone. That is why beginners need to be assured that error can be as fertile as truth. Dr Johnson was wrong about Milton's 'Lycidas', and that is more like a reason for attending to Johnson than a reason for neglecting him.

THE WRITING BLOCK

This is more vividly known as 'white-paper phobia'. It is a kind of fear, and can be prescribed for only on the assumption that it is an irrational fear; if one is genuinely incapable of writing, then no advice will help. But there are those who protest to themselves and others that they 'cannot write' even though they are in fact fully capable of writing, and know themselves to be so. The problem is not often discussed in print; perhaps the only extended account in English of what authors actually do, and how they do it, and between which meals in the day, is to be found in the first volume of Harriet Martineau's *Autobiography* (1877). But some crumbs of advice may help.

1. All beginnings are difficult. To start writing can feel like trying to start a car on a cold morning. But there is a solution to that. One can conceive the first sentence the day before, if not earlier. It is not difficult to memorise one sentence. And that would mean that on sitting down to begin, the first sentence is already there in the mind, and needs only to be written down. And once pen or typewriter is running, the worst problem may be over.

2. Fast writing can be better than slow. It can give pace to prose, and keep the connections between the arguments clear and lively. What was written fast will always need to be revised; but there is still much to be said for putting it all down rapidly and carelessly, and everything to be said for leaving the polishing to a later stage: 'raking out the clinker', as Kipling called it. Momentum must not be lost. And since revision is always easier than composition, there is every reason to make the act of composition, or the first drafting, as free-running as it can be, postponing the subtler decisions about style to another hour.

3. If you must stop in first draft, stop at a point where it will be easy to start again. It is better to interrupt oneself in mid-sentence, for this reason, than between sentences or between paragraphs.

4. People who say they cannot write often write good letters. It can release a block, then, to write an essay in the form of a letter:

Dear Mr X,
    I was reading *Macbeth* this week, and it struck me that what Macbeth does is inconsistent with what he says. If he knows he is not going to enjoy the crown when he gets it, why . . . ?

There have been critical dialogues, after all, like Plato's and Dryden's; and epistolary novels like Richardson's. The epistolary critical essay might now be usefully invented as a new literary genre.

5. Design needs to be there before you start. Writing has its own bonus system, it is true, in the form of what one thinks of inventively as one writes. But one cannot live on bonuses. The back-of-the-envelope is one excellent way of shifting the difficulty of writing to an earlier stage; so is conceiving the first sentence well in advance of writing it

down. Such notes may be of the briefest, and in a private code; they may even be mental. But they need to be there. Any writer is grateful for being able to assure himself that he does not have to say everything at once; that he can safely neglect this aspect or that for the moment, because he has dealt with it already or means to deal with it later. Notes give a linear function to one's ideas: one thing at a time.

6. To write good prose, as a famous novelist once remarked, you need a lot of luck. But you need something else as well: a sense of organisation. And in the last resort there is no one to organise a writer, that loneliest of beings, but himself. That means he must study his own temperament to discover the nature of his congenial moods. A few people, believe it or not, write best in company, such as on committees during trivial items of business, or during boring speeches; but most write best alone. Some need to feel only an hour clear before they can begin at all, others know from experience that they will need two, or even three. Some sit, some stand, some walk about the room; and a few (including Wordsworth) compose in the open air. Some write best before breakfast, others late at night, but most (and those the most sensible) between breakfast and lunch. And so on.

Nobody can answer those questions for an author but himself. He can find the answers by trying out the possibilities that there are. And when he has found them, he can arrange his day so that his chances are given free rein. A talent, as everyone knows, is not to be buried. But more than that, it needs to be studied, and even pampered. It will return the respect that is given it.

Notes for Further Reading

(Unless otherwise stated, the place of publication is London)

1 PRELIMINARY ENQUIRIES

Northrop Frye, *Anatomy of Criticism* (Princeton, 1957) is an ambitious attempt to describe literary genre, and the argument is continued in Graham Hough, *An Essay on Criticism* (1966). Lionel Trilling, *Sincerity and Authenticity* (New York, 1972) debates shifting views of the status of literature in the past two centuries; and Renford Bambrough, 'Literature and philosophy' in *Wisdom: Twelve Essays*, edited by Bambrough (Oxford, 1974) is a philosopher's view of that relation. See also under 3, below.

2 CRITICS SINCE 1920

Twentieth-century Literary Criticism: A Reader, edited by David Lodge (1972) is an anthology. On the post-war 'Age of Criticism' see John Wain, 'The Vanishing Critic' in his *A House for the Truth* (1972). The 1963 reprint of *Scrutiny* (1932–53) is indexed, and there is a *Selection*, edited by F. R. Leavis (2 vols, Cambridge, 1968). The Parisian school of Roland Barthes and others is defended by Serge Doubrovsky, *Pourquoi la nouvelle critique* (Paris, 1968), and disputed by Jonathan Culler, *Structuralist Poetics* (1975); for an anthology, see *Structuralism: A Reader*, edited by Michael Lane (1970), from Saussure to Barthes.

3 WHY LITERARY JUDGEMENTS ARE OBJECTIVE

Laurence Lerner, *The Truest Poetry* (1960) argues persuasively for the cognitive view; William Righter, *Logic and Criticism* (1963) is sceptical about the connection; see also E. D. Hirsch, *Validity of Interpretation* (New Haven, 1967). For a post-Wittgensteinian view, see John Casey, *The Language of Criticism* (1966), or Roger Scruton, *Art and Imagination*

(1974). The argument has more recently moved towards science; see Israel Scheffler, *Science and Subjectivity* (Indianapolis, 1967), and Mary Hesse, 'In Defence of Objectivity', *Proceedings of British Academy* (1972).

4   WHAT HISTORY DOES

The emergence of literary history since the eighteenth century is described in René Wellek, *The Rise of Literary History* (Chapel Hill, 1941), and its recent revival in George Watson, *The Study of Literature* (1969). The problem of the author's intention is debated in C. S. Lewis and E. M. W. Tillyard, *The Personal Heresy* (Oxford, 1939); and by W. K. Wimsatt and Monroe C. Beardsley in a 1946 article, 'The Intentional Fallacy', revised in Wimsatt, *The Verbal Icon* (Lexington, Kentucky, 1954); the debate is collected in *On Literary Intention*, edited by David Newton-de Molina (Edinburgh, 1976).

5   LANGUAGE OR LINGUISTICS

There is a collection of linguistic essays since Caxton in *The English Language*, edited by W. F. Bolton and David Crystal (2 vols, Cambridge, 1966–9). Some old books are still helpful, such as Henry Bradley, *The Making of English* (1904), a history of the language; or Ernest Weekley, *The Romance of Words* (1912); a recent equivalent is Barbara M. H. Strang, *A History of English* (1970). *Literary English since Shakespeare*, edited by George Watson (New York, 1970) is a collection on style for the literary student, from Shakespeare to the twentieth century.

Modern linguistics may be approached through an introduction like John Lyons, *Introduction to Theoretical Linguistics* (Cambridge, 1968); or through a treatise of some literary application, such as Roman Jakobson and M. Halle, *Fundamentals of Language* (The Hague, 1956). The most recent grammar of educated modern English is Randolph Quirk and Sidney Greenbaum, *A University Grammar of English* (1973, corrected 1975), a shortened version of their *A Grammar of Contemporary English* (1972). Elizabeth C. Traugott, *A History of English Syntax* (New York, 1972) is a transformational approach, its fifth chapter on 'The Development of Modern English since 1700'. Stephen Ullmann, *Language and Style* (Oxford, 1964) and *Meaning and Style* (Oxford, 1973) are well-documented collections of essays.

Meanwhile, critical studies by men of letters have continued, happily unaffected by linguistic fashions: William Empson, *The Structure of Complex Words* (1951); Donald Davie, *Articulate Energy*

(1955), on poetic syntax; C. S. Lewis, *Studies in Words* (Cambridge, 1960, enlarged 1967); and Graham Hough, *Style and Stylistics* (1969).

6 HOW TO READ: OR PRACTICAL CRITICISM

The pioneer-work, I. A. Richards, *Practical Criticism* (1929) was imitated by few before the 1940s, apart from William Empson, *Seven Types of Ambiguity* (1930, revised 1953). An American sequel was Cleanth Brooks, *The Well Wrought Urn* (New York, 1947) which followed his influential college anthology *Understanding Poetry* (New York, 1938, revised 1956) edited with Robert Penn Warren. *Interpretations*, edited by John Wain (1955, with new introduction 1972) was a British echo of the American New Criticism.

For more recent instances, see W. H. Auden's Oxford inaugural lecture, 'Making, Knowing and Judging', reprinted in his *The Dyer's Hand* (1963); Winifred M. T. Nowottny, *The Language Poets Use* (1962); and Donald Davie, *Thomas Hardy and British Poetry* (1973). There are also studies of how poems came to be written, draft by draft: M. R. Ridley, *Keats's Craftsmanship* (Oxford, 1933); Jon Stallworthy, *Vision and Revision in Yeats's Last Poems* (1969); and T. S. Eliot, *The Waste Land*, edited by Valerie Eliot (1971) with manuscript facsimile. P. J. Croft, *Autograph Poetry in the English Language* (2 vols, 1973) is the fullest study of English poetic manuscripts, with facsimiles; and *Poems and Critics*, edited by Christopher Ricks (1966) is a working anthology from Shakespeare to Hardy. The best study of literary translation is *On Translation*, edited by Reuben Brower (Cambridge, Mass., 1959).

On metre, Karl Shapiro, *A Bibliography of Modern Prosody* (Baltimore, 1948) lists studies since Saintsbury's three-volume history (1906–10), with a glossary of terms. There is a succinct account by C. T. Onions, 'Prosody', in *Cassell's Encyclopaedia of World Literature*, edited by S. H. Steinberg (1953, revised 1973), vol. 1. There is a reasoned defence of traditional against 'free' verse by Yvor Winters, 'The Influence of Meter on Poetic Convention', in his *Primitivism and Decadence* (New York, 1937), reprinted in his *In Defense of Reason* (Denver, 1947). W. K. Wimsatt, 'One Relation of Rhyme to Reason' is an original contribution based on Pope, in his *Verbal Icon* (Lexington, Kentucky, 1954), supported by his 'The Concept of Meter' in his *Hateful Contraries* (Lexington, Kentucky, 1965). R. L. Brett, *An Introduction to English Studies* (1965, revised 1976) is a booklet designed for schools and colleges.

7   HOW TO WORK: OR USING A LIBRARY
See references in text.

8   HOW TO WRITE: OR THE USE OF ENGLISH
Anthony Burgess, *Language Made Plain* (1964) is a lively primer on
writing 'for amateurs by an amateur' in matters of language, though a
professional novelist and critic. Sir Ernest Gowers, *The Complete Plain
Words* (revised by Sir Bruce Fraser 1973) is a guide for administrators
and others; and George Watson, *The Literary Thesis: A Guide to Research*
(1970) is a handbook mainly designed for those writing dissertations.
Some old books are still useful, notably Sir Herbert J. C. Grierson,
Rhetoric and English Composition (Edinburgh, 1944, revised 1945) which
deals historically with questions of style, including the choice of words
and how to build paragraphs and arguments.

Index

Acton, Lord   56
Aristotle   19
Arnold, Matthew   20, 21
assonance   87
Auden, W. H.   18, 114, 121
Austen, Jane   75, 110
Ayer, A. J.   37

Bacon, Francis   92, 93
Baker, Ernest A.   104
Bambrough, Renford   119
Beardsley, M. C.   30, 59, 120
Bentham, Jeremy   21
Berkeley, Bishop   36, 37
bibliographies   95–6, 101–2
Blake, William   82
blank verse   85–6, 88ff.
Bolton, W. F.   120
Boswell, James   103
Bradley, A. C.   47
Bradley, F. H.   29
Bradley, Henry   120
Brett, R. L.   121
Brontë, Charlotte   91
Brooks, Cleanth   27, 31, 121
Brower, Reuben A.   121
Browne, Sir Thomas   92
Browning, D. C.   105
Burgess, Anthony   122
Butler, Samuel   60
Byron, George Gordon   86, 87

Campbell, Roy   86
Carlyle, Thomas   65, 75, 82
Carroll, Lewis   49
Carter, John   101
Casey, John   119
Chambers, Robert   105
Chapman, R. W.   75, 105

Chaucer, Geoffrey   41, 69, 86
Chomsky, Noam   67ff.
Christie, Agatha   61
Cicero   47, 92
Ciceronian English   92
Coleridge, S. T.   18, 47–8, 86, 100–1, 108, 114
Conan Doyle, Sir Arthur   61
Conrad, Joseph   110
Constable, John   82
Cousin, John W.   105
Cowper, William   90
Croft, P. J.   121
Crystal, David   120
Culler, Jonathan   119

Davie, Donald   120, 121
de Beer, Esmond   103
De Quincey, Thomas   40
definition   44–5
Defoe, Daniel   109
Dickens, Charles   49, 61, 63, 75, 104
dictionaries   97ff.
Donne, John   75
Donow, H. S.   102, 103
Doubrovsky, Serge   119
Dryden, John   69, 88, 91, 92–3, 99, 114

Einstein, Albert   106–7
Eliot, T. S.   27ff., 38–9, 46, 55, 85–6, 88, 115, 121
emblems   104
Empson, William   27, 28, 52, 73–4, 120, 121
enjambement   88ff.
equality   21–2
etymology   97–8
Evelyn, John   103

feminine endings 90–1
Fielding, Henry 60
Forster, E. M. 55, 110
Fraser, Sir Bruce 122
frequency, word 103
Frye, Northrop 32, 42, 119

Gowers, Sir Ernest 122
grammar 73ff., 94
Gray, Simon 112
Gray, Thomas 76, 86
Greenbaum, Sidney 120
Grierson, Sir H. J. C. 122

Halle, M. 120
Hardy, Thomas 85, 101
Hegel 28, 29, 65
Henkel, Arthur 104
Herbert, George 87
heroic couplets 86
Hesse, Mary 120
Hirsch, E. D. 119
history, literary 31–2, 55ff., 120
Homer 39
Hooker, Richard 92, 93
Hough, Graham 119, 121
Houghton, Walter E. 104
House, Humphry 32
Housman, A. E. 52–3, 111
Hunt, Leigh 59

ideology 50ff.
indexes 103
intuition 45

Jakobson, Roman 70, 120
James, Henry 18, 32, 71, 95
James I of Scotland 87
Johnson, Samuel 18, 47, 48, 81, 99, 108, 115
Jones, L. G. 70
Joyce, James 91, 102

Keats, John 19, 20, 81
Keynes, J. M. 63
Kipling, Rudyard 116

Lane, Michael 119
language 58ff., 66ff., 120–1
Lavoisier 62
Lawrence, D. H. 33–4
Leavis, F. R. 27ff., 119
Lerner, Laurence 119

Lewis, C. S. 38–9, 46, 98, 120, 121
libraries 95ff., 122
linguistics 66ff., 120–1
Locke, John 36
Lodge, David 119
Lovejoy, Arthur O. 32
Lyons, John 120
Lysenko 50

Malory, Sir Thomas 74, 102
Marlowe, Christopher 85, 88–9
Martineau, Harriet 116
Marvell, Andrew 98
Marx, Karl 37, 50, 52, 56, 64–5
masculine endings 90–1
memory 19–20, 109–10
Mendelssohn 40
metre 85ff., 121
Mill, John Stuart 52
Milton, John 38–9, 60, 62, 75, 85, 87, 88, 90, 93
Monro, Hector 59
moral criticism 20–1, 30

Namier, Sir Lewis 56
New Criticism 25ff.
Newton-de Molina, David 120
nominality 111, 112
nonsense 58–60
Notes and Queries 100
Nouvelle Critique 33, 34, 42
novels 104
Nowottny, W. M. T. 121

objectivism 15–16, 19, 35ff., 119–20
Onions, C. T. 69, 96, 121
Orwell, George 49, 53, 64, 111, 112
ottava rima 86–7
Oxford English Dictionary 67ff., 96, 97ff.

Patmore, Coventry 59
periodicals 104
Petrarch 87
philology 73ff.
Pierce, G. A. 104
Pinter, Harold 71
Plato 21, 64–5
Pope, Alexander 86, 91, 99
Popper, Sir Karl 46
Positivism 37–9, 56
Powell, L. F. 103
practical criticism 57, 81ff., 121
prose 91ff.

Protagoras   36, 37
proverbs   103–4
punctuation   108–9
Purdy, Richard L.   101

Quirk, Randolph   120
quotations   109–10

Ransom, John Crowe   26, 27
rhyme royal   86–7
Richards, I. A.   27ff., 83, 121
Richardson, Samuel   60, 102
Ricks, Christopher   121
Ridley, M. R.   121
Righter, William   119
Russell, Bertrand   63

Sader, Marion   104
Sainte-Beuve, C. A.   57
Saintsbury, George   32, 57
Saussure, Ferdinand de   67
Scheffler, Israel   120
Schöne, A.   104
Scrutiny   21, 27, 30, 119
Scruton, Roger   119
Senecan English   92
Shakespeare, William   17, 20, 61, 63,
   68, 74, 75, 76, 81–2, 85, 87, 88–90,
   98–9, 103, 112, 114, 116
Shapiro, Karl   121
Shaw, G. Bernard   109
Shelley, P. B.   85
Short-title Catalogue   102
Sidney, Sir Philip   87, 108
Smith, Sydney   108
sonnet   87
spelling   106
Spenser, Edmund   63, 86–7, 99
Stallworthy, Jon   121
Steinberg, S. H.   121
Sterne, Laurence   18, 36–7
Strang, Barbara M. H.   120
structuralism   67ff., 99–100

style   110ff.
subjectivism   15–16, 31, 33–4, 35ff.
syntax   88ff.

Tate, Allen   27
Taylor, Jeremy   92
Tennyson, Alfred   86
tense   74–5
theory, literary   42–3
Thomas, Dylan   71, 76, 87
Tilley, Morris P.   103
Tillyard, E. M. W.   120
titles   109
Tolkien, J. R. R.   100
Tolstoy, Leo   35, 53
tragedy   42–4
Traugott, Elizabeth C.   120
Trilling, Lionel   32, 119

Ullmann, Stephen   120

Valéry, Paul   71
verse   84ff.
vocabulary   75, 113

Wain, John   119, 121
Warren, Robert Penn   27, 31, 121
Watson, George   120, 122
Waugh, Evelyn   108
Weekley, Ernest   120
Wellek, René   120
Wilson, Angus   71
Wilson, F. P.   104
Wimsatt, W. K.   27, 30, 120, 121
Wing, Donald   102
Winters, Yvor   121
Wordsworth, William   20, 41, 43, 51,
   60, 75, 81, 82, 90, 109, 117
writing   106ff.; writing block   115ff.
Wyatt, Sir Thomas   87

Yeats, W. B.   63